I Stake My Claim

Rev. Wiley E. Shelton

I Stake My Claim

Reverend Wiley E. Shelby

Electric Tactics

Monroe, Michigan

I Stake My Claim

ISBN: 978-0-9830859-2-8

Library of Congress Control Number: 2017964202

All Bible quotations are from the King James Version.

We are grateful to the copyright owners for permission to use the following material:

Newspaper clippings are from Knoxville News Sentinel, © 1940-1984, Jack McElroy, editor.

 "I'm Gonna March" © 2018 by Charles Shelby.

"Hunting" © 1995 by Stephen Shelby.

 "Mark's Story" © 2014 by Mark Shelby.

 "Giving Thanks for God and Country" © 2017 by G Stanford Pierce, Sr.

"The Seer of Bethlehem" © 2018 by Stephen Shelby.

"I Stake My Claim" © 2018 by Dwayne Shelby.

Photograph "Shelby Family 1952" © 1952 by Bob Courtney.

Cover illustration, "Wiley Shelby Contemplating", and "I Stake My Claim" drawings by Cassandra Stetson

Contents

ACKNOWLEDGEMENTS

Thanks to many who helped make this book a reality.

My daughter, Debbie Godfrey, has worked on my book for years with edits, rewrites, more changes and additions. About the time she thought it was finished, I gave her additional sheets to further explain an incident or some forgotten detail that God brought to mind that helps tell my story. Debbie has enjoyed the journey and knows that God's glory will be shown through her efforts. To God be the glory!

My step-daughter, Sandra Turner, whose talent with computer research and email correspondence to verify sources and obtain reprint permissions made the final few months of this project less stressful.

My step-son, Mark Johansen, formatted the book for printing and assisted with the mechanics of publication.

My wife, Ruth Shelby, spent many hours proof-reading and making corrections.

I Stake My Claim

By Dwayne Shelby

A wealthy man in the Bible
Had all things that this ole world could give
He didn't have compassion
The kind of love God gives you
When you know Him.
But a beggar on the streets
So hungry his body filled with pain
Had much more wealth in Heaven
On the wings of an Angel made his claim.

I stake my claim in the blood that flows from Calvary
And the promises that God gave to you and me.
No more wandering about
Now I'm sure without a doubt
That on the gold streets of Glory
I'll stake my claim.

For a long time I wandered
Aimlessly without a single trace
That just up ahead of me
I'd soon find that perfect grace-filled place.
It was there God's son was sacrificed
By my sin and he died without blame
So at the foot of Calvary's hill
There I knelt and staked my claim.

Wiley Shelby

INTRODUCTION

From early childhood, I thought that God might want me to preach someday. If I could just be the kind of preacher—like that old country preacher that I was saved under his preaching—that would please God and be alright with me. But as I grew older, other things filled my life. In 1945 it was the army. Even with all the GI's there, I felt alone. With fear and a heavy heart, I told God I would do whatever He wanted me to do if He would take me safely home to my family. In August 1946, God did just that. But I was in no big hurry to find out what God had in store for me to do. We went to church, but weren't involved. God got my attention around 1947. He reminded me of my promise, so I began by teaching a Sunday School class of Junior boys. I sang in the choir. Then I began to grow in grace and knowledge.

In 1961, I was ordained as a deacon in Brushy Valley Community Baptist Church in Tennessee. Then in 1962, I was ordained as a Baptist minister at Emmanuel Baptist Church in Anderson County. Souls were saved, Christians rededicated their lives to God and the church began to grow. I had found my life's purpose. During those seven years at Emmanuel, four young preachers came out of that small congregation. There is no absolute record of how many others made Christian commitments and continued serving God in various aspects of their lives; but the revelation is definite—God specifically chose me, just as well as others, to do a good work. Who would have thought that I would be chosen to preach the Gospel?

I accepted God's call to minister. My work involves me with the poor to middle class, often in rural areas but then back to the inner city. I always wind up in a struggling smaller church that needs to grow and has nowhere else to go but up. It became obvious to me that God uses me to provide hope, comfort, and spiritual guidance for a particular audience, those who may not be touched by the ministry of larger, "organized" religion.

Accepting the call to Christian ministry, no matter what form it takes (pastor, pastoral care, youth leader, missionary, minister of music, church or service leader) requires a great personal commitment and a lifelong relationship with Christ. "It ain't easy" nor is it impossible! As Paul said, no matter what circumstance I find myself: "I can do all things through Christ which strengtheneth me." (Philippians 4:13)

The rough journey I began smoothed with the realization that I am intentionally part of God's plan. As I look back, significant events helped to shape my ministry and continue to lead me down particular paths: sometimes sweet, often painful, but always accompanying spiritual growth. God is the source of my strength.

The spiritual journey becomes sweet when we can completely depend on and trust God. No job is too difficult. My desire is to prompt readers to accept the call to work for the Kingdom of God, to pursue God's direction, to realize personal potential, to face the challenge head-on, and to commit to Christ for the long-term. Through this book, I'll attempt to offer nurturing for spiritual growth, strength for perseverance, and help for building confidence to go forward.

I knew from an early age that I would write a book one day. As I grew up, I would record life's events on scraps of paper, on napkins, on the back of envelopes, on anything I could find at the time. Then I would squirrel these bits of paper away, knowing someday I would return to them. The time has finally come! All of those bits of scribbled memories have finally come together.

I have many good reasons to write this book:

- To bring encouragement and support to one who might be struggling with decisions about entering ministry work.

- To encourage the reader to discover their own purpose in life and to step out in faith to accomplish that purpose.

- To encourage the reader to make a strong commitment to faith and to run that race with excellence.

- But after all is said and done, my greatest purpose in writing this book, as in every endeavor of my life, is to bring honor and glory to the Lord Jesus Christ, on who's Word I stake my claim.

To everything there is a season, and a time to every purpose under the heaven:

A time to be born, and a time to die; a time to plant, and a time to pluck up that which is planted;

A time to kill, and a time to heal; a time to break down, and a time to build up;

A time to weep, and a time to laugh; a time to mourn, and a time to dance;

A time to cast away stones, and a time to gather stones together; a time to embrace, and a time to refrain from embracing;

A time to get, and a time to lose; a time to keep, and a time to cast away;

A time to rend, and a time to sew; a time to keep silence, and a time to speak;

A time to love, and a time to hate; a time of war, and a time of peace.

What profit hath he that worketh in that wherein he laboureth?

I have seen the travail, which God hath given to the sons of men to be exercised in it.

He hath made every thing beautiful in His time: also He hath set the world in their heart, so that no man can find out the work that God maketh from the beginning to the end.

Part I: A Preacher's Life

CHAPTER 1. PREPARING SOIL IN GOD'S GARDEN

A time to plant, and a time to pluck up that which is planted

It was cold and rainy as we left Knoxville in 1929 to move to our ninety-six acre farm in Union County Tennessee. We piled into the front seat of a 1927 Chevy touring car for our big move: my Dad, James Elbert Shelby; my Mom, Francis Mae; five-year-old brother LeRoy; baby sisters Bertha Mae (age 2) and Isabell (age 1); and me the three year old. The back seat of the car had been removed to accommodate our cherished hog. My older brother James, age 8, preferred to ride in the moving van rather than squeeze in with us—and the hog.

Somewhere in the valley near the Baptist Church, the moving van got stuck in a muddy crater called Byrams Fork Road. The movers worked desperately to free the van, but after several unsuccessful attempts decided to give up and spend the night there in the van. Our family proceeded in the cold dreary weather to the big but cozy-feeling farmhouse that would be our new home.

Through the rain, we could barely see the large country porch wrapping around three sides of the farmhouse. We entered down a long hallway with six or seven rooms extending right and left from it. Dad built a fire in the fireplace in one of the huge rooms while Mom placed a pile of soft straw on the floor. We snuggled together dreaming up countless adventures that would become lasting memories.

Memories? Yes, but no bathroom! The outhouse was about two or three hundred feet from the main house in a field. "Running water" meant we **ran** to fill a bucket at the cistern in back of the house. (The cistern collected rainwater from the gutters.) After a couple of years, we had a two hundred-foot deep well dug about twenty feet from the house. Ah, how we enjoyed the taste of cold refreshing limestone water from that well. Dad even installed a new-fangled, "Sears and Roebuck Red-jacket Hand Pump"!

During these Depression years, Dad said he had to keep his job at the Knoxville newspaper until the farm became profitable. For a while, he drove the thirty-five miles daily over dirt country roads to earn enough income to support our growing family. Slowly the farm began to show progress from all our hard labor. While he went to his day job, we still had our chores to do; such as feed and water the animals, chop wood for heating and cooking, etc. We had a couple of cows, hogs, chicken and a team of plow horses. Farm work was hard work for a mere boy!

At about seven years old, I learned just how difficult farm work could be. Dad had plowed the field but the dirt clods were so hard that the turning plow could not break the dry ground suitable for planting. Leroy and I got the job of chopping the clods with a fork hoe. Naturally, I wanted to play and explore—not break up clods!

Annoyed at having to work, all my anger was directed at those dirt clods like they were my worst enemy. This was not my idea of a fun day. My wildly flailing hoe pounded the hard earth. In fact, so hard was my pounding that the hoe's prongs bounced off target right into my poor foot! With blood gushing and me wailing, Dad gathered me up to the house for his doctoring methods. His "doctoring" was almost as painful as the accident. To stop the bleeding, Dad made a mixture of coal oil (kerosene) and salt, packed together with lard, and applied it to the wound. He lovingly wrapped it with bandage but sent me right straight back out there to finish my chore and think about controlling my temper!

It took a long time to heal and left a neat scar the size of the end of my finger. I'm not convinced of the healing power of "coal oil" but the kerosene worked well in our lamps for light. There was no electricity out in the country. Kerosene was five cents per gallon and often hard to find. Up the road about a half-mile was Sam Campbell's store where we got the kerosene. Sam allowed us to swap our eggs or butter for things we couldn't grow, like sugar, salt, baking soda, or baking powder. Today that's called bartering; back then it was survival.

Besides eggs and butter, we raised other essential crops on our farm like corn for livestock feed and bread. Corn is a great example of hard work on the farm: planting, harvesting, shucking and shelling. About once a month, Dad and James (my oldest sibling) would load a sack of corn on one of the horses to take to Alvice Ridenour's mill. Ridenour would trade a peck of some produce in exchange for grinding our corn into meal.

After a couple of years, Dad decided that he could build a mill to grind corn for himself. He had finally acquired and set up all the necessary parts for a working mill. It worked for a while--but then the old motor he used broke down. Next, he rigged his car motor to do the job! Dad jacked up the back wheels and ran the belt to grind the meal. This worked temporarily. Then one day, as he was grinding, he reached through the car to adjust the belts. His shirt became entangled and the mill pulled him into the machine. This almost killed him! For quite some time he was unable to do much work, so he closed his mill down and got rid of the equipment.

A time to be born and a time to die

After the mill grinder incident, our family faced even more difficult times ahead. The Great Depression spread as our family grew and finances tightened. We moved out of the farmhouse into a small four-room house. On August 31, 1938, Mr. & Mrs. George H. Snodderly sold us 40 acres for $300. My oldest brother, James, left home to get out on his own. He lived with relatives and took a job in North Carolina.

In those days, families were expected to have several children to have help with farm work. My parents suffered the loss of two babies early in their marriage. But Ms. Cooper, the midwife, was called to deliver four more: Lassie, T.J. (Ted), Paris Edgar, and Samuel Sterling were born. Then Bobby Gene came in 1937. By 1939 the thirteenth child, Mary Ann was born.

Late in 1939, four of us had double pneumonia. Back in Union County in those days we didn't have many doctors. I was thirteen years old and Lassie was seven. We were deathly ill but survived the sickness. Yet, three-month old Mary Ann and six year old Paris Edgar died within three days of each other. Neighbors came from miles around to help the Shelbys during this awful time. Some friends brought food; others cut wood or helped with chores; some just sat up at night caring for our sick. I can remember the load of commodities being delivered from the County Seat of Maynardville. Somehow, I knew we were loved.

We put up vegetables on our farm in the fall. It was rough. I can remember sometimes my dad, Leroy, and I would walk down to Norris Lake about ½ mile from our house. The lake was backed up from Norris Dam. Before daylight we would wade out into the lake and used our home-made gigs to spear the fish and a grass sack to carry the fish back to the house to cook. The fish were spawning there in the weeds. Even the carp fish were good to eat.

It was a bad winter, 1940. We lived in a four room house with weather board, no insulation. We had a pot-bellied stove for heat, that didn't heat the house very well, and we had a wood-burning stove to cook on.

There was mom and dad and nine of us children, ages 13 down to 3 months. Each one knew what their job was and took care of it. Sometimes we got along and sometimes we fought like other siblings.

I have wondered, since I got older, whether my mom and dad losing the children so close together may have partly brought on his problems. This was 3 months before the tragedy.

A time to laugh

Times got better, even though we were still "as poor as old Job's turkey." Tradition held an important place in our lives. Saturday or Sunday evenings would be reserved for our family croquet game. One minute we were playing together, the next minute, like most siblings—fighting together.

Christmas provided a special family time. The annual ritual involved chopping down the "right" Christmas tree and decorating it with strings of popcorn. The night before Christmas, each child marked his/her name on a newspaper page and placed it near the tree, anticipating a great surprise on Christmas morning. There were always gifts of fruit and candy, but one year I got a French harp (harmonica) *and* a striking pair of cotton gloves with yellow tassels dangling from stiff cuffs—very stylish!

Leroy and I spent most of our time together, probably because of our closeness in age. We explored caves and collected bags of Indian arrowheads. Often we hiked along the back ridge behind our farm looking for "mountain tea" or Teaberry. These leaves were especially tasty to chew.

We set rabbit traps in winter. The first catch was always our dinner. We killed, cleaned, and skinned them. Any additional catch of the day was taken to Sam Campbell's store to sell in Knoxville. As the law required, we left one foot un-skinned so buyers would know it was rabbit, not cat. Sam got us fifteen cents for each rabbit. We saved enough money from this lucrative enterprise to buy us each a pair of thirty-five cent brown cotton gloves. We sure were proud of those gloves because we bought them ourselves.

The rabbit trapping business fell by the way as Leroy and I became excellent hunters. Now we added squirrel, opossum, and turtle to our family's dinner menu. My mother, being part Cherokee Indian, could make a good meal out of whatever we brought in to her. She knew which weeds or wild greens were suitable to cook for dinner, such as narrow-dock, spotted-dock, spider leg, and phantom dandelion. Many times, I helped pick wild greens for dinner. My older sisters were expected to help with the cooking, cleaning, and caring for the younger siblings.

Berry picking was part of our childhood adventures. Leroy and I allowed Bertha Mae and Isabell to accompany us to the berry patch. With buckets in hand, we sent the dogs ahead to scare out the snakes. Snakes were a threat to us, but for our two sisters it seemed that bugs were just as threatening! Leroy and I were obliged to tease them with bugs as often as possible. Laughing, playing and eating, we filled our buckets: One berry for the bucket—one for the mouth, until both were full. What a pleasant, rewarding chore!

Bertha Mae and Isabell walked to school with us too. Central View School was a little white two-room building at the top of Big Ridge. The school was about three miles east of where we lived, in Blue Mud Valley. There were no school buses in this rural area so we met other children along the route. It seemed the Shelby kids were prime targets for chiding and bullying by other kids.

Leroy and I could tease our sisters but other kids could not!

On the second day of school that year, the Allread brothers, Roy and Johnny began picking on Bertha and Isabell. It was getting a little too rough—so the fight was on! Leroy held Roy so I would have perfect aim at his posterior. I used my extremely thick geography book to whack his bottom a few times to teach him a lesson. Needless to say, that lesson taught me some things too. After facing the school principal over the fight, swift and certain punishment would surely follow at home. Dad had laid down the rules to us with no exceptions. It wasn't the fight or even misusing the book that got me in trouble. The rule was clear: If you get a whipping at school, you get another one at home.

Lunchtime was usually a real social event at Central View. One day, I poked my head into a circle of kids gathered on the playground just in time to see Leroy and Junior Settles exchanging punches. Just as I posed my head for the perfect view over a friend's shoulder, Junior let me have the fist to the nose meant for Leroy. I backed out faster than I went in—that dizzy feeling, with eyes watering, nose throbbing—I had seen enough, in fact all I could take. The next morning, I awoke with black eyes and a red nose fit for a clown. Dad's rule kicked in again. But this time I got three whippings: Junior, Principal Weaver, and Dad!

Central View's Principal, George Weaver, was a pillar of the community and also the song leader at Byrams Fork Baptist Church. This was the church where I was saved from my sin by the grace of God. At age eleven, I didn't know much about worldly sin but this church had a preacher that taught me about my personal sin. Clem Cooper, a tall skinny man of God, preached about "hell-hot and heaven-sweet." This was what some people called a "hellfire and damnation preacher." I can't remember the sermon topic that Sunday morning but I do remember his wife coming to me and inviting me to the altar to pray. (In 1937, Clem's wife was the attending midwife as my mother gave birth to my brother, Bobby Gene. All these years later, it is on this page that Bobby Gene will learn that it was I who asked momma to give him that name. He hated his name for years, thinking it sounded too much like a girl's name. Of course, it did not help that momma originally spelled it "Bobby Jean"!)

As I went to the altar, I didn't know what to do or how to pray. I watched as other Christians prayed. Then I began to talk to God, too. "LORD, I know you can save me. You saved my brother!" As soon as these words came out of my mouth, I felt as light as a feather and knew that the LORD had come into my heart. I felt clean. I couldn't wait to get home to tell my mother what had happened. Many times before that time I thought I was saved. This time it was different. I realized that if I could be a preacher like Clem Cooper, it would be all right with me!

A time to mourn

As kids, we scoured the area caves looking for arrowheads and old Indian relics. There was an area of about eight or ten acres of bottom land where Byrams Fork Creek ran through an open field. Byrams Fork Road was on one side and a big ridge (now Big Ridge State Park area) on the other side. Most of my collection came from the Big Ridge area. The last time I saw my collection was in a large brown paper bag at Grandpa Sterling Smith's smokehouse in 1940. That's where we went when my parents began having marital problems.

There were times when Dad would fly into a rage, but I guess most of us are guilty of that if we don't turn our problems over to God. Dad went to church only a couple of times that I can remember. I had been told that perhaps some of his problems came after being shell-shocked and gassed during World War I.

In 1916, my Dad, James Elbert Shelby, age twenty-one, married Frances Mae (Fanny) Smith, age fourteen. Fourteen months later, Daddy was inducted into the army to serve as a machine gunner with the Thirtieth Division. His military papers describe him as a twenty-two year old farmer with blue eyes, brown hair, ruddy complexion, standing 5'7" tall. He received a Bronze Victory Button for his service, including operations and attacks in Belgium, Hindenburg, Bellicourt, Hauroy, Part of Bony, Brancourt, Bremont, Busigny, Vau Audigne, St. Soaplet, Sell River and Magingheim. He was honorably discharged on March 5, 1919. This seems like a lot of action in a short period of time. So maybe some of his problems did start from the war days?

Fast-forward to 1940, Mom left Dad with kids in tow to stay with Grandpa Smith. After a few days there, Bertha Mae, Isabell and I somehow wound up staying with my oldest brother James in Knoxville. James and his wife Marie lived in a three-room house on Lonas Road; three siblings joined them as they were expecting their first child. You just did what you had to do to make things work.

While living with my brother James and his wife, I got a job nearby in Mr. Cole's grape vineyard. I was not yet fourteen when Bertha Mae delivered the wretched news of my parents' death to me right there in the vineyard.

Dad was served divorce papers and devised a horrific plan. Since he didn't even own a gun, Dad went to a neighbor asking to borrow one to kill some rats on the farm. I can remember one of my neighbors commenting, "I could hear him firing the gun so he must have been target practicing."

It was June 26, 1940, when Mom and the younger children were staying at Uncle John Gray's house on Alice Bell Road just outside the Knoxville City limits. Dad arrived at the location to convince her to drop the divorce proceedings and come home. They argued; he pulled the gun and unloaded six bullets into my mother. He then ran into the woods behind the house and reloaded. The newspaper reported, "...the law and a posse of neighbors went to hunt him down." As they closed in, Dad shot himself, one bullet to the head. In his pockets, they found some money, not much; each size bill was folded separately and in different pockets. By this, they assumed he had planned to leave town.

After their double funeral Grandpa Smith was appointed administrator of the estate and guardian of the children. Since there wasn't much of an estate to handle, the real job became what to do with seven children. In just a few days, he began to dole out the children and scatter my family to different homes. Perhaps he thought he could not provide for us all and that we would have a better chance, financially, if we were split up.

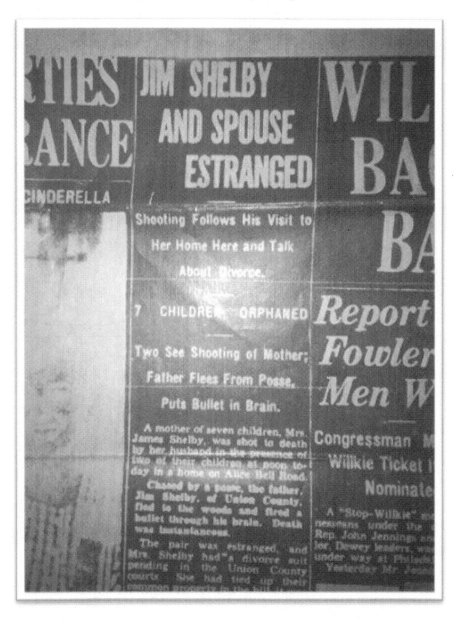

Farmer Slays Wife, Self Here

Two of Jim Shelby's own children were on the premises yesterday when he shot and killed their mother. They are in the picture along with other children. Front row, left to right, are Bobby Gene Shelby, 3, J. B. Gray, 8, Louise Gray, 10. In the rear are T. J. Shelby, 5, and Lorrene Gray, 14, only eye-witness to the murder. Shelby later committed suicide.

CHAPTER 2. NURTURING A YOUNG WEAK SPROUT

A time to heal

I was placed in the home of Gerty Irwin. Gerty must have been fifty-five or sixty at this time and lived with her thirty year old son Joe. They both seemed old to me. Their farm was between Andersonville and Big Ridge, partly in Anderson County and partly in Union County. I was terribly unhappy!

I found myself living with two total strangers. I wanted to go home. I missed my family! I felt so alone, so homesick, so depressed. I just knew I was going to die. I remember being sick for several days. Gerty finally contacted Grandpa Smith asking him to come talk to me. He visited for a while, but then left me there! I guess he thought I probably wouldn't die. I recall his encouragement, "You don't die from being homesick. Besides, there are plenty of chores to do on this farm and school starts in just a few days."

By the grace of God, I did survive and did start school again. Andersonville School soon started, where I began to meet new friends. The school was huge! Quite different from the last school I had attended. This was a two-story building with classes upstairs, a lunchroom, an auditorium and a huge gymnasium. I couldn't believe that students were allowed to rollerskate on the hardwood floors. I tried it... first and last time. I spent more time on my seat than on my feet! Skating was not for me so I tried out for the basketball team.

Since I was rather large for my age, I made the basketball team, playing center most of the time. Mr. Claude Sharp, the principal, was also the coach and my eighth grade teacher. I'm convinced that God must have placed him there for me as my major influence during that devastating readjustment year.

It was about a mile walk to the school bus stop. The ride was only four miles to school so I often chose to ride my bike instead of taking the bus. Besides, I was proud of my used bike that I had bought with money from my new job, after school and chores were done. Mr. John Fogarty hired me to work at the Hilltop Restaurant. (To me it seemed more like the local beer joint.) Because of my young age, I couldn't work behind the counter selling alcohol. Most of my time was spent in the kitchen learning to cook, usually by "trial and error". After our regular customers had a few too many beers, I realized they really didn't care if I was a good cook or not. So I experimented using a pinch of this and a bit of that until I was satisfied with the result.

As I recall, Mr. Fogarty's driver had an artificial leg. This was interesting to me since he seemed to have no difficulty driving the A-Model Ford for Mr. Fogarty. One particular day, Mr. Fogarty was irritated that his driver was not available. He urgently needed to see Urt Carroll over at Dark Hollow so he asked, "Could you drive me?" Are you kidding? What an opportunity! I had only driven around the parking lot a few times, moving the car back or forth out of the way. To say the least, I was inexperienced. My reply, "Sure, I could do that but I don't have a license."

So we started down the road across from Norris Lake at Andersonville Boat Dock. Not a mile down the rocky crooked road, we happened upon a state road crew working to repair the roads in one of the sharp S-curves. Suddenly a heavy construction truck backed right off a bank into the passenger side of Mr. Fogarty's fine car. No one was hurt, just damage to that lovely A-Model Ford. The job foreman took all the pertinent information so the State of Tennessee could pay for the car repair. Next day, that same foreman visited Mr. Fogarty with the promise that "the state will fix the car but may also be pressing charges because your driver was driving without a license." Mr. Fogarty decided the damages were really not that bad. "Just forget all about that," he replied.

I continued to work at the restaurant after school and on Saturday through graduation. I bought myself a brand new green pinstriped suit to wear to my Eighth Grade Graduation. It didn't cost that much but I was proud that I bought it myself. As I walked across the stage to receive my diploma, I felt like I was ready to take on the whole world.

SCHOOL DAYS
1940 - 41

A time to Love

After graduating, I left the Irwin's farm heading for Knoxville. My Uncle Ed Smith allowed me to stay with him and Aunt Peggy at 909 Richard Street. Since I had no money, I had to begin looking for a job. However, at age fifteen, no companies would hire me without a work permit. So Uncle Ed escorted me downtown, explained to authorities that I had completed the eighth grade, and that I needed a job. With the permit, I soon found work on a lunch wagon owned by Tom Comer. The lunch wagon was located at the Brookside Cotton Mill. I was paid to make sandwiches and push the cart through each department, selling sandwiches, cakes, candy and soft drinks.

This job went well for a few weeks, until I came in a few minutes late one morning. Mr. Comer became outraged that I would be even five minutes late. He further accused me of being out drunk the night before. That set me off! He couldn't talk to me like that! I had worked around alcohol, didn't like anything about it, and absolutely did not even touch the stuff! One word led to another. He mentioned firing me and of course, I took the opportunity to say, "You can't fire me. I already quit!" ...and I walked out.

Soon, I had a new job at the Western Avenue Market, Sparks and Brews Restaurant. Now I worked behind the counter and sometimes helped in the kitchen. I enjoyed working there because of the variety of people I met. Some were tobacco farmers auctioning goods at market. Others were produce farmers, interstate haulers, or grocers, but there was one particular dairyman that I "took a liken to."

The dairyman was none other than Mr. Frank Weigel. (I'm sure he would be proud of the Weigel's Convenience Stores on almost every corner in Tennessee today.) He wore overalls and didn't appear to me as a man with lots of money. He didn't treat me like a poor little orphan boy either. Maybe he liked me because I was a farm boy. Anyway, Mr. Weigel impressed me every time we talked. I think the success of his business had a lot to do with how he treated people. To me, he was the best example I had ever seen of a really "good" man.

Business slacked off and I was out of work again. Since Uncle Ed had a good job at Huber & Huber Transfer, he helped me get work on their loading dock. I was still living with Uncle Ed and Aunt Peggy the first time I met the future Mrs. Wiley Shelby. If I live to be a hundred, I will never forget that day...or that night!

Saturday, January 29, 1943. As Aunt Peggy and I were walking the three blocks home from the drugstore, we decided to stop in at the Galo Ice Cream Parlor on Fifth Avenue for a milkshake. A beautiful young blonde waitress came over to our booth. It was definitely "love-at-first-sight." I knew that she was meant for me. Handing her a dollar, my opening line was, "Can you give me some nickels to play the jukebox?" She brought back five nickels and three quarters and sweetly asked, "Is that enough?" Of course, I took this to be flirtation...and the courtship began!

Aunt Peggy and I left the Ice Cream Parlor at about three o'clock in the afternoon. After walking about a block, I turned to her and declared, "She (the waitress) is my woman even if I never get her." She said, "What?" I repeated, "That's my woman, if I never get her." She said, "You are crazy." I said, "No I'm not. I know what I'm talking about." All afternoon, I could think of nothing but that beautiful girl. I didn't even know her name! I had to go back that very day to find out. It was about eight o'clock in the evening when I arrived back at the Galo. The beautiful dream was gone! After a bit of conversation with the owner, Pop Greer, I learned her name was Imogene and she had gone to a late movie at the Strand Theater. They were showing "Little Tokyo USA." I caught the next street car heading downtown.

When I arrived at the Strand, the movie had not started. I purchased a ticket and a bag of popcorn, surveyed the theater, and spotted my dream girl. The best viewing seat for me just happened to be a couple of rows behind Imogene and her family (Aunt Pearl, Uncle Bill, and sisters Katherine and Maggie, and Maggie's boyfriend Speedy Galloway).

 She didn't appear to notice me. In an awkward attempt to get her attention, I threw popcorn at her beautiful flowing hair until she looked around for the nuisance. I waited a few moments and started throwing popcorn again. For a while she brushed popcorn out of her hair. Then she turned around and looked as though she was angry. I motioned for her to come and sit with me. She shook her head no and gestured for me to come and sit with her ... and her family. So I jumped over the seat and sat next to her.

After the movie, I asked to see her home. Since I had no car, she asked her Uncle Bill to allow me to ride with them. Uncle Bill said, "I guess it will be all right. He looks like a nice fellow." (Thus started a new direction and purpose in my life.)

The next day we had our first official date: a nice Sunday afternoon stroll for just the **four** of us—Imogene, me, and Imogene's sisters Katherine and Maggie. We had a wonderful leisurely walk across the Oak Street Viaduct, up Henley Street, across the bridge over the Tennessee River and back. I can't remember ever dating Imogene without her sisters, who always seemed to tag along. Our Sunday afternoons were filled with long walks, to Fountain City or down Kingston Pike. Sometimes we just went for a milkshake to the Western Avenue Drugstore or Courtesy Drugstore on Gay Street.

We had been dating a few weeks when Pop Greer told Imogene she had to work on her scheduled day off. She demanded to be off. He told her she would work when he said she would work—and besides ours "was only puppy love that would be over in a few days." She refused to work. He fired her! That puppy love lasted over 70 years. Looking back, I can see that God placed Imogene in my life that day.

After about three months of dating, I asked Imogene to marry me. She talked to her father about this. He didn't say, "Let's talk to your mother about this." He actually said, "You will have to get permission from your older sister Katherine." Finally he approved of the marriage if we set the date on his birthday August 4. So, we began making wedding plans.

August 4, 1943 came quickly. Getting married was not a simple task for this young couple. I would not turn seventeen until August 19. My bride was six months younger than me. First was the blood test, then three days of waiting before a marriage license could be issued. Since we were under the legal age for marriage, Imogene with her dad and I with my older brother had to appear before the Juvenile Court for approval. Judge Webster peered over his horn-rimmed glasses and growled down at us, "Don't you kids know that you ought to be in school?" I was sweating his decision but he finally gave us the okay.

Preacher Henry Maples performed the ceremony in Imogene's living room at 1219 West Fourth Avenue. Surrounded by our family, with Kathryn as Bridesmaid and James as Best Man, we became husband and wife. We had a lovely wedding dinner hosted by neighbors, Mr. & Mrs. Arnold Dicks. Then off to spend our first night together—with James and Marie Shelby, in their home on Middlebrook Pike (a three room house with a one-hole outhouse 100 feet from the back door.)

Three days after our wedding, we went on our honeymoon—to Union County Tennessee. We rode the Grey Hound Bus Line to Highway 33 at Hickory Star Road. About 2:30 PM, we started walking to Hickory Valley Road, about a quarter-mile past the Hickory Valley School (or Old Buccaneers School). It was a rocky road, no black top surface! Back then, not many cars traveled this path. My bride had worn high-heal shoes at first, but then pulled them off, laughed a while, and cried a while. It was after dark when we arrived at my Grandpa Smith's home. He and his wife were already in bed. We were offered no supper but I doubt we would have eaten even if they offered something. Come to find out, my grandpa had just been married to his new bride, Bell, for only a few days!

Imogene and I saved $600 from the time I proposed. We rented a house at 909 West Fourth Avenue and bought adequate furniture. My new father-in-law proposed that we go into business together since I had restaurant experience and he knew the perfect location. He invested $500 in war bonds and we invested our remaining savings in this venture. In just a short time, while I was still just 17, we had a thriving business, S&J Café (Shelby & Johnson), at the corner of North Central and Bernard Street.

Our café was open twenty-four hours every day. The Oak Ridge plant was thriving so our business was good. My father-in-law George and his daughter Katherine worked the day shift with a cook named Kate Coffee. Imogene and I worked the night shift and we were not happy. It seemed like we were spending all our time at the restaurant and putting all our money back into the business. Things were not going well so we decided to sell our part of the business to her dad for nearly nothing. We just wanted out of the restaurant business and to get on with our life.

For the next eleven months, I dug ditches, unstopped sewers, or drove the truck for Roy White Plumbing Company. At wages of $1.82 per hour, we had enough money for a couple of week's groceries. Just like in the depression movies, I received "Greetings from the President of the United States." Here I was barely eighteen years old, still a boy. My number came up so I had to go. Once again, I felt the pain of being stripped of my family. In January 1944, I left my wife and four-month old baby George to serve my country.

A time of war and a time of peace

Lord, I know you will not give me more than I can handle…

But I just wish you didn't trust me so much!

About the time we sold our share in the restaurant, my eighteen-year-old brother Leroy was drafted into the Navy. He wrote me letters often during his time in service; but I missed him so much. His rank was Seaman First Class USNR. His job was tail-gunner on the destroyer ship, USS LUCE. It had made several trips back and forth to Germany during the war. This was their first trip starting to go to Japan.

My induction had taken place at the army base in Fort Oglethorpe, Georgia. After three days, they moved me to Fort McPherson. A few more days passed when I boarded a train to Camp Joseph T. Roberson, in Arkansas for my basic training.

Then a suicide bomber hit my brother's ship eleven miles off Okinawa, flying right into his gun crew—killing them all. I got the letter informing me of the devastation and Leroy's Purple Heart. I loved him but I also know I will see him again one day. I am confident Leroy is with the Lord.

By early June, I returned to that train station in Little Rock to greet my family. As I surveyed the train station, I was expecting to see my wife carrying our little baby, George. To my surprise there was a nine-month old toddler walking between benches, accompanied by Imogene, Uncle Bill and Aunt Pearl Housewright. I didn't even recognize my son!

We rented a room for a week in "The Levy", a neighborhood in Little Rock, Arkansas. Housing was hard to find during World War II, so after a week my family went back home. After my basic training, I got a furlough to go home. But the joy of going home was overshadowed by the expectation that when I returned to duty I would probably be shipped overseas. Of course the Lord was watching over me, as I should have known!

There I was standing in line with gear in hand waiting for the trucks to take us to the train station—when the order came for me to stay put. (This happened twice so I know that God was in control of my orders.) Because of my kitchen experience, I was instructed to report to a different company on the other side of camp.

My kitchen experience had not included cooking for over 250 men at one meal! As Private First Class, I was assigned to the position of Second Cook for a short time. Then I was promoted to First Cook and Tech Corporal. It didn't take long to move up the ranks to Tech Sergeant, then Mess Sergeant. I went on furlough expecting to be made Master Sergeant when I returned to my mess hall. However, while I was away they moved in a Master Sergeant with eighteen years of service into "**my**" mess hall!

When I returned to base, the Captain called me into his office to warn me that I could either work with this new Master Sergeant or I could go back to cooking. I heeded his warning and just went back to cooking.

One of my fellow cooks was taken to the hospital so I found myself slicing bread in his place. I accidently nearly cut my finger off! The Master Sergeant said, "You did that on purpose so you could get out of work!" Needless to say, I had to show him that I could still work. I picked up the closest meat cleaver and chased him out of **my** mess hall. Then I found myself back in the Captains office for another not-so-friendly chat. This time he gave me another choice, "You can either apologize or you can face court-martial!" My **sincerest** apology followed...

I rented a place on North McKinley Avenue from Mr. & Mrs. Ernie Sinkerow so my wife and son could join me. It was a bedroom with kitchen and living room privileges. My army pay was not enough to pay the rent so I worked with Mr. Sinkerow building houses when I could get off base. The first week Imogene joined me, my entire company was restricted to the base. I was sweating that out but she stayed about six months. Next, we found out Camp Robertson was being shut down. I was being moved to Fort Knox, Kentucky, assigned to a tank division. The first of August, I was moved again to Fort Bragg, North Carolina for my discharge. I believe that was the longest four days I served.

Leroy's Purple Heart

Leroy

ARMY WAR BOND CLUB
HEADQUARTERS, RECEPTION CENTER
FORT McPHERSON, GEORGIA

DATE **15 Jan 45**

THIS CERTIFIES THAT:

1426 S. C. U.

Wiley E Shelby   44 068 465

HAS AUTHORIZED A MONTHLY CLASS B DEDUCTION
TO COVER PURCHASE OF A UNITED STATES WAR BOND.
HE IS THEREFORE ENTITLED TO
MEMBERSHIP IN THE ARMY WAR BOND CLUB.

COMMANDING

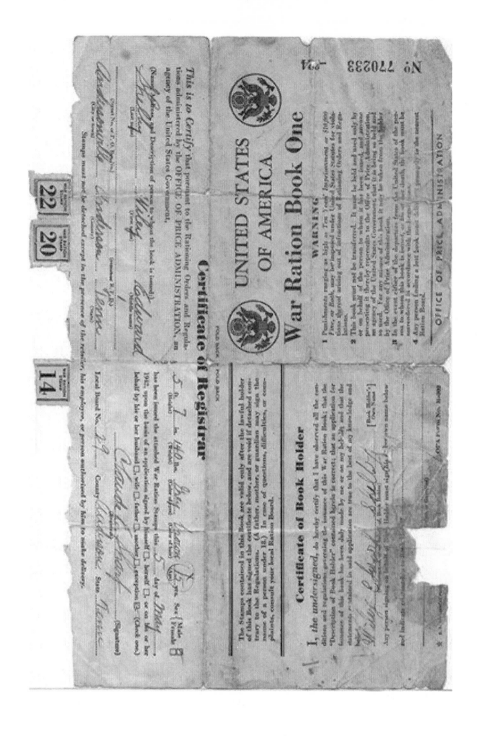

WW2 Ration Book

CHAPTER 3. DEVELOPING STRONG CHRISTIAN ROOTS

A time to cast away stones, and a time to gather stones together

Finally back home, we moved into two rooms upstairs at my in-law's house. It was another difficult transition time. I suffered nightmares for a while. (Now I think they would call it Post Traumatic Stress Syndrome.) One night, I hit the headboard of the bed, bruising my hand. After another nightmare, I had a hard time explaining how I could hit Imogene with my fist in my sleep. The worst was probably when she woke me just as I was attempting to climb out the upstairs window while sleepwalking!

I tried to return to my old job at Roy White Plumbing Company. Mr. White was out of town. The manager in his absence, Mr. Abe Ogle said, "You don't have a job here anymore. Mr. White is not going to hire you back." I knew legally when a person was drafted into the military, his job was held for his return. The lady at the draft board suggested I could just go to work at the White Store, making about the same wages. I said, "No, I want my $1.82 per hour job back that I had just like the law says." She picked up the phone, called Mr. Ogle and asked, "Is Mr. White in business to stay in business?" He answered, "Why yes!" Then she proceeded to give him her name at draft board # 50, "If he wants to stay in business, then he better put Mr. Shelby back to work soon." I believe that was on Friday. By Monday, they sent someone to tell me to go to work that day.

Our second son Charles was born. By nine months old, he became sickly. Dr. Black made several house calls to see him. This time he said he had done all he could do. "The rest is up to a higher power." Dr. Black had no idea what was wrong but suggested we throw out our portable oil heater. He would rather we had no heat than to have that heat source.

I knew what part of the problem was. I had made a promise to God that if he would send me back home safely to my wife and baby I would do whatever He wanted me to do. But I had not kept my vow to God. I wasn't doing anything "bad," I just wasn't doing **anything**. I was not attending church, nor witnessing, nor anything else like I knew a Christian should be doing. When the doctor said those words "done all I can do", my eyes were opened. I knew it was time for me to keep the promises I had made in the army. I found a quiet place to pray.

As I began to take part in church work, we saw a great change in our baby's health. The more I did, the healthier Charles became. I taught Sunday School, became Sunday School Superintendent, accepted Trustee and additional offices in the church. I always felt like God was preparing me for ministry.

In spring of 1948, we found and fell in love with a little four-room house on Virginia Avenue. It was eleven months old, no trees, no flowers but plenty of knee-high weeds. I knew God had to be in the arrangements because everything went so smoothly. My GI loan was approved through Home Federal and we moved in by June. Things seemed to be going well for us.

Charles was getting better. We had bought our own home. I took my exam for a plumbing license. (Mr. Frank White, the city plumbing inspector, kidded me that the paper was to draw pipes, "not rivers and streams." But He gave me 90 on the test and I received my license.) I had graduated from apprenticeship to journeyman plumber through Plumbers & Steamfitters Local Union #102. That meant more money to live on.

We even bought a car. I had received $400 for "mustering out" pay upon discharge from the army. I used that to buy a 1936 Plymouth with a 1939 motor. It wasn't much but a way to get to work, church, and shopping. It had good tires. This was important since tires, along with a lot of other things, were still being rationed from the war days.

I continued to work for Roy White until 1950. We had four boys by this time, George, Charles, Gary and Stephen. Then I went to work at Oak Ridge Building K29. I worked with a man named Snodderly, who gave me a wonderful recipe for a No-Bake Fruitcake. When you say "fruitcake" a lot of people snarl their nose. But, this is more like candy instead of cake. I have made this cake at least a couple of times every year since then, for Thanksgiving and Christmas. I've mailed it to other states and countries, like Hawaii and Turkey. It is heavy to ship but even soldiers and marines have enjoyed it. I can't remember missing a year since I started making it!

No Bake Fruitcake Recipe

16 oz box graham crackers, crushed (save the box)

8 oz black raisins

8 oz white raisins

1 cup English walnuts, chopped

16 oz candied fruit and peel mixture

4 oz candied cherries

16 oz marshmallows

12 oz can evaporated milk

Before you start preparing ingredients, cut and line the graham cracker box <u>first</u> because mixture will set up fast. Lay box flat on table; cut the broad side of box top on three sides with knife. Raise the top lid and line the box with wax paper.

In a large bowl, mix crushed graham crackers, raisins, nuts, fruit, and cherries. In a saucepan, combine marshmallows and milk, cooking over low heat. Stir continuously until completely melted. Pour marshmallow mixture over the dry ingredients, stirring with a spoon until coated. Cool until you are able to work the mixture with absolutely CLEAN hands. (Don't forget to check for clean fingernails.) If the mixture sticks to your hands, try adding a little water to keep it moist.

Press fruitcake mixture into the shape of the lined graham cracker box. Optional: press more nuts and cherries on top as decoration. Refrigerate overnight and rewrap in foil. Allow two days to set up before serving. (Will keep at least 2 weeks in refrigerator if wrapped.)

When K29 was finished we moved on to Building K31. I worked in many areas out there in Oak Ridge. Seems like I would work a few months, get laid off for a few months; then get sent to another location. That was the way it was in construction. When you finished a job, you were laid off until the next job started up. It was hard work but honest work!

Through the years, I would be out of work for up to four or five months at a time. I had offers to go out of Tennessee to a job but never left my family. I had heard about families being split up after these jobs. I loved my family so much that I couldn't chance this. I could have gone where the money was and not been there for my family as they were growing up. But I remembered being a teenager without a dad or mom. So I put my faith in God, trusting Him to supply our needs.

There were times when I was out of work and money was low, wondering what I was going to do. One time, groceries were almost gone. I was getting worried and began to pray. Early the next morning, I walked out to the edge of our yard and there next to the street lay a $10 bill. All I could say was, "Thank you God for placing this here." Our street was not well traveled and we had had no visitors. I must admit it surprised me even though I had quoted Psalm 37:25 many times: "I have been young, and now am old; yet have I not seen the righteous forsaken, nor his seed begging bread."

Early in our marriage, Imogene and I had been baptized at the same time at Northside Baptist Church. Preacher Maples said that He felt it would be good for us to be baptized together since we were so young, and he had joined us in Holy Matrimony. As I look back, I think it was a wonderful start of our Christian walk and our married life so close together. After I was discharged from military service, we joined West Side Baptist. We were the Christian type that went to church whenever we felt like it. Then the Lord reminded me of the vows I had made to Him. We began to work on having our family in church and Sunday School on a regular basis!

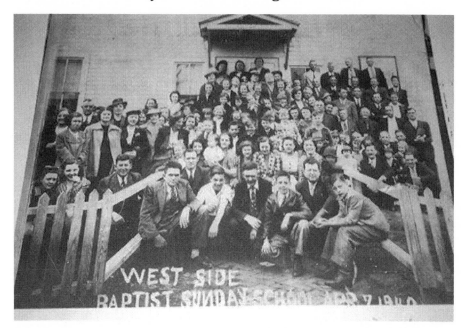

West Side would have to move since the new highway was taking that property. We (the Trustees) found and bought a 3-room house on Vermont Avenue where I started holding Sunday School. We cleaned it, did a little work, put in a piano, some chairs, songbooks, and Christian literature. Seems like we had twenty or thirty regular attendees. Then we went back to services at the original church while they tore down the house to start the new church building. There was more to church than the building!

In the 1950's, some of us young folks from the church would have a "cottage prayer meeting" in someone's home. We met two or three times per month. Something you don't hear much about these days. People would invite us into their homes where there were lost or sick. We were just doing what the Lord said to do; taking the message to them. This was our way of going to the "hedges and highways" with the Word. We even had tent revivals and open-air meetings in back yards. We were seeing souls saved and enjoying the Old Time Gospel in song and preached Word.

My Brother-in-law, Carl Knight, took on a little church in Brushy Valley as pastor. He wanted me to lead the singing there! We enjoyed many good experiences there as the people felt the power of the Holy Spirit. Back then, they were not ashamed to shout and praise the Lord.

One night in Brushy Valley Community Baptist Church, some young people were on the altar. One young man got up and walked out the door during prayer. I remember praying for him asking God to stop him, send him back inside, and save him before it was too late. In just a few minutes, the young man came running through the church doors to the altar. He fell on his knees and before long came up to announce that God had saved him.

During the time I served there as deacon and song leader with Preacher Carl, we were also on the radio on Saturday from 3:00 to 3:30 PM. Carl soon gave up the broadcast but I continued for sixteen years. God was blessing the radio ministry and I was enjoying it. My daughter Debbie played the piano for us until in 1972 she got married and her husband was relocated with the army. The week she was to leave, I worried, "Who will play for the broadcast on Saturday?" My son Mike volunteered, "Daddy, I will play for you." I didn't take him seriously because he had never had piano lessons.

He had sat with Debbie and watched her play, maybe even striking a few notes. But I had no idea he could play like he did!

As Saturday approached, I was moping around worried about the broadcast. Mike reminded me, "I told you I will play the piano on Saturday for you." I said, "You really mean that, don't you? Well okay then." When the time came, he played like God had poured it out on him. Within the next few days we lined up a piano teacher for him to take proper lessons. After four or five lessons, the teacher told my wife there was no need for him to come for lessons, because everything she put in front of him he could play. I thanked God for supplying our needs and Mike's talent!

In 1962, Emmanuel Baptist Church of Anderson County called me as their pastor. I was ordained and began my ministry to the little flock. God began to bless us as several souls were saved and many rededicated their lives to God. The church grew as God continued to bless it. At least three or four young preachers came out of that church. We have many fond memories from pastoring there for seven years!

One favorite memory: I would gather the small children as the service began to teach them a song or scripture lesson so parents could see their darlings in action. One particular Sunday shortly after Christmas, I asked them if they had a song that they would like us to sing. One little fellow, while adjusting his cap gun in his holster shouted, "Sing Pistol Packing Mama!" Lesson that day was Proverbs 3:6 "In *all* thy ways acknowledge him…"

My wife would line our children up on the pew beside her, just within reach, to keep them quiet during services. While I preached messages, Charles would entertain the rest of the family by drawing pictures to illustrate my sermons. This time it included a foot, labeling it as "Noah's Ark and My Arch". He was listening... Children will listen and learn in their own way. Sometimes we could learn a few things from them too.

At one time, I just was not enjoying my Christian life. I guess I was lazy or the devil was after me. I think I had a vision because I don't think I was asleep. In the vision, I saw a beautiful white building on a hill. A man stood in the front archway to the building. I stood on a hill across a valley from the building. I could not see the man as plainly as I wanted to but I thought it was Christ Jesus. A voice spoke to me with clear instructions, "Move up a little closer." I moved toward the building until I could see that it was my LORD. Then I knew my problem. I would enjoy serving Him more if I would only move closer to God, spiritually.

Some may think things just happen, but God has a purpose for all things. Shortly after this experience, Martin Luther King was assassinated. Our Country's social problems got worse. Even locally, cars were being turned over and rocked to spread fear. My family was out for a drive, about to cross the railroad tracks at Western Avenue and Keith Street. In front of me, a carload of men stopped abruptly and slung open all four doors at once. The men bailed out and approached my car. I began calling on God for His help and mercy. My wife was terrified and also called on the LORD! Our children began to cry with fear. That day, God was with us. The men got within a few feet of my car but did not touch it. I don't know what God showed them but they ran back to their car, slammed the doors and left in a hurry. I thank God and praise Him, for I know it was God that sent those men away. He does answer our prayers and He will take care of His children.

In 1969, I was called to pastor Bethany Baptist Church on New York Avenue. Attendance was very low; even members were not attending like they should. We worked for a while: visiting, praying, and getting members to do the same. After a while it began to build up. I had heard that a new family just moved into the neighborhood from the country. I could see the house, yard, and their dogs from the church steps. Since I knew someone was home, I decided to visit in between Sunday School and Church service. I almost got to their door when the two dogs put me at bay. The door was cracked open about two inches, but no one responded to my knocks or the barking, biting dogs. The dogs were shaking my pant-legs like a rag, but nobody came to my rescue! I made it out of the yard without too much damage. That is enough to make a preacher stop visiting. But God said to go! And finally those good folks began to attend church.

Also while at Bethany, our church was set on fire by a sixteen-year old boy. About four o'clock in the morning, he had broken in to steal an amplifier not even worth $25 at the time. To cover his tracks, he set a bag on fire in the basement. By the time I got the call, the fire department had saved over half of the building. However, smoke and water damage claimed most of the furnishings. The next Sunday was Easter Morning Sunrise Service held on the church's front lawn. All of us were feeling low but we trusted God to bring us restoration.

From that point, we got permission to use Lonsdale Elementary School until the church was renovated. It took several months and lots of hard work to find a contractor, repair the building, clean the furniture, etc... The boy basically got a smack on the hand and no help for the church. But we read Romans 12:19, God said, "Vengeance is mine, I will repay." On Judgment day, the boy will stand before God, just as each one of us.

I was at Bethany for about seven years. The church was looking good. Folks were enjoying the services. God was blessing us. I believed my work was done there, so I gave it up and went back to West Side, my home church. Here, I worked with these good folks while waiting upon God to send me to pastor another church.

I waited two years before being called to pastor Bon View Baptist on Belleaire Avenue. This was in the Beaumont area where my children all went to elementary school. Now it was 1978. God had given me a place to work with a new congregation. As with every church I pastored, there were some problems. The congregation was scattered and very few were attending. But as we began to work and pray together, God began to bless our church. Everyone was doing their part and we enjoyed seeing it grow both in number and spiritually. We enjoyed about as good a choir as could be found in any church. If you think I am bragging, I am! Bragging on what God does, not what man does.

I was so happy, about that time, because all my grown children were attending church, somewhere, most every time Sunday came around. Even those who were working out of town, on jobs where they had to work some Sundays, would go to church when they could.

But now, it bothers me that some don't attend very often. I know God said, "Those whom I love, I rebuke and chasten." And when he whips His children it hurts for a long time. In Revelation 3:19, God said, "As many as I love, **I rebuke** and chasten: be zealous therefore, and repent."

After leaving Bon View Church, I returned to West Side, my beloved home church. Then the folks at Elm Street Baptist Church sent me word to fill in while they were searching for a pastor. Then they stopped looking for a pastor and I stayed there, trying to serve and preach the word of God.

It seemed like everything I tried to do just would not work. Satan was always on his job, but I also knew that my LORD said, "Lo, I am with you always, even to the end of the world," and "I will never leave thee, nor forsake thee." (Matthew 28:20; Hebrews 13:5)

I often talked to God about it until I finally felt I had received the answer to my prayers. After serving there about five years, one day from the pulpit, I resigned effective immediately and returned to serve God in my home church. I had not quit working for God. I was waiting for the LORD to show me what he wanted me to do next. There is always work to do. I am worshipping Him. I continue to praise Him. I continue to serve Him:

whether through teaching a Sunday School class once or twice a month, singing in the choir most every Sunday, singing solos for Him, leading the song service on Wednesday nights, praying for others, and always listening to God. Even with all this work to be done, I missed being a pastor. Like the prophets I ask, "How can I not talk about Him, when He has done so much for me? But his Word was in mine heart as a burning fire shut up in my bones, and I was weary with forbearing, and I could not stay." (Jeremiah 20:9)

A time to rend and a time to sew

In 1981 my health began to fail me. If it wasn't ulcers, it was respiratory or prostate or some other problem. The list went on: Bronchitis, hiatal hernia, diverticulosis, and asbestosis, to name a few. I had pneumonia again, the eighth time in my life. By 1989, I was still having health issues.

I blacked out a couple of times. Imogene heard me hit the floor in the bathroom at home. When we got to Dr. Bunn's office, he sent me directly to Baptist Hospital Emergency Department with instructions, "Do not stop for anything! They will have a wheelchair ready for you and put you in the intensive care unit." My blood count had dropped to 29 when it was tested. That time, I spent two weeks in intensive care then was sent to a private room. The second night in the private room, the nurse checked me about 11 PM. Again, my blood count had dropped so low they started two units of blood. They couldn't seem to find where my blood was going. One doctor suggested that my body was absorbing it.

At that time, I was working as a plumber/steamfitter at Y-12 Oak Ridge National Laboratory. I blacked out again, this time at work. They called the ambulance, began giving me oxygen, checked me at Medic to stabilize me then transported me to Methodist Medical Center. Later that day they moved me to St. Mary's Hospital in Knoxville so I could be closer to my family.

Two of the doctors that day said I had had a heart attack. So, in a few days, I was on the treadmill test. The technician there said I had at least one blocked artery. The Cardiologist reading my chart disagreed, "You were probably having angina pains." They suggested I carry glycerin pills to put under my tongue if I had pain in my chest or arms.

Still trying to work until I could retire at age 65, I had another spell on the job. This time when my blood count dropped they called in more specialists. I had two bone marrow tests, which were no fun at all. The first was 1981 when a class of 8-10 nurses and techs enjoyed studying me and poking me. This time only the necessary medical team was present. For a while they thought it was leukemia. Finally a blood specialist came in to diagnose the problem as ITP (Idiopathic thrombocytopenic purpura), a rare disorder affecting platelets. We were told the treatment required a very expensive medicine that insurance may not cover. Imogene told the doctor if I needed it and insurance didn't pay, we would get the money somewhere. I can recall the urgency in his diagnosis, "This usually takes three separate dosages but you need it right now and it will cost $5,000. We don't need to wait."

The specialist turned to my wife, "It will take a few minutes to prepare the medicine. I want you to stay by his side while it goes in his arm. It will take four hours and you can't leave his side for one minute until it is all gone." Imogene stayed by my side, the nurses checked in every few minutes, and all went well.

Feeling somewhat better after this ordeal, I planned to return to work. Since I was still employed at Oak Ridge National Laboratory, I returned for my first day back. I entered the security gate that morning with no problem. However, leaving that afternoon was a different story. As I stepped into the gate area, I set off the alarm system. With bells ringing, lights flashing, and whistles blowing, security guards swarmed around me with guns drawn. It nearly scared me to death. I didn't know what was going on. Security searched my lunchbox and me from top to bottom, turned my pockets inside out, took off my hardhat, checked the band in it, ran a Geiger counter over me, and asked me to remove my shirt and shoes. All this, while questioning me about where I had been while I was absent from work. For three hours they held me to make sure I wasn't contaminated with radiation.

After explaining about being in the hospital, they had to confirm it. I was instructed to bring a letter from the attending doctor detailing the medicine I had received. Also, I would be required to carry that letter with me to gain access through the gate in order to work.

I continued working for a little longer, trying to reach retirement age. I began having breathing issues, got tired easily and other health problems. Work was getting slow. It was hard for me to give a good day's work. So at age 63 and a half, I decided to take a cut in my social security check and "go on and hang it up." Fishing and hunting would take up more of my time. I thought I might even get Imogene interested in fishing so she would go with me! (I guess I was wrong to think she would like fishing even if I baited her hook.) I never seemed to spend as much time as I would like on either of these hobbies.

I have another hobby: I like to work with wood, making small things. I have repaired some furniture and made some.

I made one piece I am particularly proud of. I call it a "two liter cabinet". It holds twelve two-liter Coke bottles. In the bottom part it has a counter top and above that a two-door cabinet which could hold glasses. My wife used it for medicine as we both take so many prescriptions. This whole top part could be slid off and put on a counter top.

I am also proud of some of the bathroom caddies I made. One type was for two rolls of paper, a hair drier, curling iron, brush, and comb.

I made another for toilet paper and books. It has a heart-shaped base. Another one sits on the floor, about 12 x 12. It has space for spare paper, two side posts, and two book shelves. At the top is a paper roller with a 10 x 10 heart at the back of the holder.

One type I made was in the shape of a toilet bowl, with the tank and toilet seat, that pulls up and it stores toilet paper in it.

There was one that I made from a croquet ball and a round piece of wood at the floor and a dowel. It made a place for three extra rolls of tissue paper. I guess being a plumber for 50 years still showed up in my projects even after I retired.

I enjoyed taking parts of an old table some friends of mine had thrown out in the trash. I salvaged the legs and the top, and I then put ceramic tile on it. I gave it back to them and they were thrilled. As far as I know, they used it for years in their dining room.

I have made several things and gave them to family members.

One of my daughters-in-law and two grandkids wanted me to make them a toy box. I asked, "How big?" She said, "Pretty big." The toys were scattered all over the place so I made a BIG box to put in their room. So I began to plan what I thought would be nice. I put a desktop lid and bench and two handles to pull out on each end. It looked like a construction gang's toolbox. When I got done it was just about that big. When I took it to them, it just fit in the door.

Another time one of my sons got a large piece of furniture from a garage sale. It was so big that I had to take it apart piece by piece so I could work on it. I cleaned it up and repaired all the bad parts. It looked so bad he said he didn't want it. I think they called it a secretary and wardrobe. About a year later I got it finished. One of my daughters-in-law fell in love with it. I gave it to her. She went to an antique dealer and bought another piece go to with it.

I didn't make any money at my hobby, but I think I made some people happy.

That is what life is all about. You don't have to be an old grouch because you are up in age! One thing my hobby does is keep me out from under my wife's feet so we are not barking at each other all the time. They say, "True love doesn't run smooth." Ours must be the genuine thing for sure. Sometimes the road is very rough, even after 50 some years, but it's worth every pebble that your bare feet step on. So maybe some day you and yours can look back and see it wasn't so bad after all, because it takes both of you to make it there and beyond. When you both have the third party, Jesus, in your heart you must let Him lead in everything you both do. You will be in the mountain sometimes and sometimes in the valley. One thing about it you can go over the rough places together. For you see, we made a vow to each other when we got married, and so did the Lord. He said, "I will never leave you nor forsake you, but go on to the end of the world with you." What makes it so bad when we leave Him out of our plans and go our own way is that it won't work. When we let Jesus have control of our lives we can look forward to see the inheritance Peter spoke about in 1 Peter 1.

Let me share a few words about that. You see, when we are born again, we become join heirs with Jesus Christ. He became the means of our salvation through His death and resurrection. You see, we have a lively hope, not a dead one, for He lives. I know I have a better home after this life is over, for Jesus said in John 14 that He was going to prepare a place for me and He would be coming after me. Peter was speaking about an inheritance that awaits me that cannot be corrupted. It is undefiled. It will not fade away. It is eternal. It is reserved in Heaven for me. I am kept by the power of God through faith unto salvation, ready to be with Him when He comes.

Sometimes we may lose sight of Heaven for a short time by becoming totally consumed by things of this world, such as fine cars, homes, money, jobs, or social standards. None of these are really bad or evil, but they can become like little gods in our lives if we are not careful. God is to be #1 in our lives, not things of this world. When we remember that nothing can separate us from the love of God after we are born again, no one can pluck us out of His hands, neither height or depth, principalities or power, can separate us from the love of God. We have a heavenly home that Paul said, "Eye hath not seen, nor ear heard, neither have entered into the heart of man, the things which God hath prepared for them that love him." (1 Corinthians 2:9)

CHAPTER 4. NOURISHMENT FOR CONTINUED GROWTH

A time to break down and a time to build up

My family threw me a wonderful surprise retirement party at Mynatt Park Pavilion in Gatlinburg. July 1, 1989 was probably the best Saturday I ever had in all the years I worked. The covered pavilion was all decorated like a birthday party. Folks brought in all kinds of food, a huge cake, many different desserts, Kool-aide, lemonade, tea, coffee. Kids and people everywhere, but only 49 signed the guestbook. We ate awhile, talked awhile, ate awhile, played games awhile, then ate again and started all over.

With Grandkids at 1989 Retirement party in Gatlinburg

We didn't have a lot of money but God gave us seven wonderful children, a roof over our head, food and clothing, and love for each other. Music seemed to be a common chord in our family. My sons were all in the high school band, blowing some kind of horn. As they learned to play their instruments, I wondered if our neighbors would run us off the hill where we lived. Soon, they began to make music. I had never thought I would like brass bands but it was wonderful. We proudly attended their concerts. Although it was costly, especially when they went on such trips as Washington's Cherry Blossom Festival Parade or New Orleans' Mardi Gras Parade. We were concerned about them when they were on the road but we raised them in church and knew that God would watch over them. We prayed for each one, day and night. What could be better? I'm still proud. We raised all seven with none of them ending up in jail or prison. I firmly believe that if I live for Him that He will take care even down to the third generation.

So blessed with a big family of seven children! I rejoice when I consider how God has used and blessed my family. Each child was so different in personality and interests, but the common threads appear to be love for Christ, family, and music. They have always brought joy, fulfillment, and a sense of pride to our home. My prayer is that the Shelby legacy continues into future generations as children of God.

A small child in church for the first time watched as the ushers passed the offering plate. When they neared his pew, he piped up so that everyone could here: "Don't pay for me Daddy, I'm under five." (Source Unknown)

According to his teachers at Beaumont Elementary School, George was a genius and because of his high IQ he should be tested further. We decided against that because we wanted him to have a normal happy childhood. He loved the band, so in the fourth grade he began playing the trombone. He became Drum Major at Rule High School during his last two years there. During High School, he worked at Minhinnett's Grocery on afternoons and Saturdays. After graduating, he worked as an announcer at WKXV Radio Station. In 1962, George joined the army and served overseas in Turkey. When he returned to Knoxville, he married Gladys Wampler and finished his military service in Arizona. After discharge, George worked his way to management at General Shale Brick Company. George and Gladys moved to Douglasville, Georgia where they raised three wonderful children of their own. George has since retired to become a farmer and is surrounded by many grandchildren. His loving wife Gladys passed away in 2016, leaving several grandchildren and great-grandchildren.

Imogene and George

Charles was the independent one, always on the move. As I described before, we almost lost him when he was a baby. He made good grades at Beaumont and also started band in the 4th grade, playing saxophone. He also became Drum Major while at Rule High until he graduated in 1965. In his last semesters of high school, he often showed up at home in the early afternoons. The teachers said he was so "high-spirited" that he needed thirty to forty minutes outside to unwind. He was always on the go. In fact, one day he broke his leg playing football. Someone said he ran into the building, others said he kicked the wall instead of the ball. After graduation, he met Faye Richards at the church where I was pastor at the time. After a few months of courting, they married. I performed the ceremony. He got a job at Miller's Department Store. They told him he would be sweeping the floors. He said that wasn't for him... Next went to work at Southern Linen as truck driver. Then to management positions at General Shale Brick, Glenn Gary Brick, and Franklin Brick.

The job at Franklin shows his determination and driving energy! The company was losing money and offered him six months to start making money or the job would end. From there, the company returned to making a profit, so Charles went on to become the president and CEO. He moved his family from place to place finally settling around Nashville, Tennessee.

Charles was always interested in planes. As kids they sat and watched them come and go. He loved fast cars and motorcycles.

A friend had an airplane. He took Charles up in it. That clinched it.

In 1970, he got a learners permit in Indiana. Some time later he got an instructors certificate in Tennessee.

He always loved to teach people new things. Part of his life was teaching. It brought great satisfaction. He opened his own aviation school in 1984, called Mid Tennessee Aviation.

His wife Faye ran the office and took care of the books. Ten instructors reported to her. She kept schedules and paid bills and keep mechanics working while Charles was working for the brick company.

One day he took me up in a little Cessna. He flew me around a pattern for about seven minutes when the turbulence hit. I was scared to death thinking the bottom dropped out of the plane. That was two rides for me: First and Last.

Charles had a brain tumor removed in 1987, hence gave up the aviation business. However, after healing from that ordeal, his pilot's license was reinstated.

Charles and Faye produced five beautiful children who now have their own children and grandchildren.

I'm Gonna March

(Words and music written by Charles E. Shelby)

Chorus:

I'm gonna march, march, march to heaven's shore.

I'm gonna sing His praise forever more!

I'm gonna sing and shout and tell the world about...

I'm gonna march, march, march to heaven's shore!

I'm gonna march, march, march every day.

I'm gonna march until I hear my Savior say,

"Oh well now, welcome in my good and faithful friend!"

I'm gonna march, march, march to heaven's shore!

I'm gonna march, march, march for God each day.

I'm gonna march until I reach the pearly gate.

I'm gonna enter that door and then I'll march forever more.

I'm gonna march, march, march to heaven's shore!

I'm gonna carry His sword and bear His cross.

I'm gonna do my part to save the lost,

Cause Jesus saved me from sin and I know I'll enter in!

I'm gonna march, march, march to heaven's shore!

Gary was the good-natured middle son. At sixteen months old, he made the news with Mamaw Johnson after swallowing a 4-penny nail and passing it! Imogene was visiting a neighbor while their porch was under construction. No one saw Gary with the nail but he began to choke. Mother's intuition kicked in so they took Gary to Knoxville General Hospital for x-rays. The doctor decided to feed him cornbread with macaroni & cheese to see if they could bind the nail and pass it instead of doing surgery. We watched every diaper change, until there it was. I kept the nail as a souvenir. He also ate Coal from the coal bucket and even swallowed a penny.

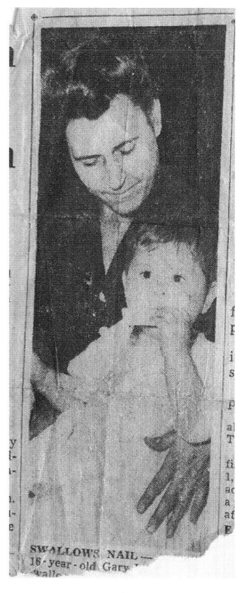

SWALLOWS NAIL —
16-year-old Gary

Gary played the trumpet and French horn in the band. He went to data processing school to learn about computers, then became a plumber like his dad, at Local 102. After several years, he became a qualified teacher for instrumentations and air conditioning. He married Carol Hobbs and they raised three handsome boys who now have children and grandchildren. They divorced and he later married Becky Darboian and they are active in church-work. And of course, he has the God-given talent of singing!

Even as a small boy, Steve enjoyed nature and showed signs of what we could expect for him as an avid outdoorsman. He would sit on the porch at night pointing out stars and naming the constellations. As a child, the only thing that scared him was his immunization shots. (He always passed out when they administered his shots.) He played the trombone in the high school band. Then after graduating from Rule High, he married Charlotte McFarland, having known her from Emmanuel Baptist Church where I served as pastor. They married while he was a marine and lived in Hawaii until his military discharge. Steve graduated from the University of Tennessee at Knoxville in accounting and worked in Oak Ridge until early retirement. Together, Steve and Charlotte have two beautiful daughters, four grandchildren, traveled the world, hiked the Appalachian Trail, Pacific Rim Trail, Everglades, England, Scotland, Ireland, Nepal, Africa, and more. Thanks to God, Steve survived and fully recovered from a horrible tree accident that almost took his life.

Steve accomplished so much and has a variety of interests and talents! He is a philosopher, writer, poet, musician, hunter, hiker, etc... Over the years, we shared many hunting trips together in God's beautiful creation. From this deep thinker comes beautiful words and works!

Hunting

(written by Stephen V. Shelby, November 17, 1995)
Frosty leaves crackle beneath my aged boots
and sparkle
As countless gemstones born
in the moonlight of an early autumn morn.
Angel-hair webs caress my face
Conceived in the architect's mind
To snare his prey
That he might live another day.
Solomon's mentor in the dark
Flies above my head and settles on decaying core
Coughs up the bones and fur from bounty
Reaped upon the forest floor.
Bobtailed lady screams
And neck-hairs stand taut in ovation,
A celebration of feast of fawn
As hint of pink applauds arrival of the early dawn.

Streaks of red and silver explode across the wooded knoll.
Cotton-ball bounces
Red and silver pounces
Breakfast is had on edge of homey hole.
Beyond the trees a monarch leaves
His lofty throne nearby
To pluck a multicolored rainbow
from a sapphire nether sky.
I take my stand among nature.
To watch, to hear, to smell

Life to give,
To take, to live.
A fat doe approaches, drifting quietly,
Munching on sweet white oak cake.
I will not take her,
Nor the scruffy offspring in her wake.
Silent and unmoving I sit against the tree
As the babe approaches unaware.
I could pet him, I could get him.
Mama snorts, stamps her foot and with flags aloft they flee.
I do not need them for food,
Though she would be tasty and he a tender treat.
For food I have enough and could well exist
with naught but butcher's meat.
The silly cow that stands and lets the sledge
Fall on his head
Sustains the life yet not the soul
Both must be surely fed.
There! Among the shadows!
Was it movement or a past
When man was one with all
And life was meant to last?
Flick of ear, swish of tail,
Steps upon the trail.
Swallow hard and surging heartbeat pounds within my ears.
Will he hear?

Or see the shaking of my hands as I raise
My trusty Remington, scarred and battered
From taking and giving life
Over many, many days.
I peer at majesty.
A regal crown proclaims his domination.
This is my need.
With soft click I remove the safety from his life
And silently plead.
He is alert now. Head and tail high,
Muscles quivering,
Fear or understanding?
I center on his chest and he must die.
Two leaps,
A fall
Some thrashing,
And he is mine.
Gently I stroke his soft coat
And look into his clouding eye
Peacefully thanking God
For life.
For God is a mighty hunter, too.
Seeking righteous souls.
Giving life and taking life
And loving life His goal.
I heft my blade and pierce his soft belly,
Cutting just beneath the skin,
And feel the gaze
of countless spirits of old and ancient men.

And reach within his bloody depths
To pull the steaming entrails free
And know the touch
Of countless spirits merging there with me.
I dare not waste a single morsel
Of this blessed day
For giving life and taking life
Is simply nature's way.
With rifle on my shoulder
I drag the prize along
A smile upon a heart
That for now can know no wrong.
Angel-hair webs
caress my face
And ahead
The architect feeds the tiny wren.
Frosty leaves crackle beneath my aged boots
And sparkle as countless gemstones die
In the sunlight
Of an early autumn eve.

Our only daughter, Debbie was born November 27, 1952. She seemed to always be in a hurry and on the go. Like her brothers before her, she was born at home. Unlike the boys, she got there before the doctor could arrive. At two years old, we found her two doors up the street, visiting neighbors. She could get out of your sight in no time flat. At three years old, she had climbed to the top of the 10-foot tree looking into our kitchen window. In 1957, while Imogene was in the hospital with sciatica nerve problem, Aunt Georgia brought Debbie to the hospital emergency department. Debbie had bounced over the side of her bed into the floor, cracked her collarbone. Now I had two in there, spending day and night at the hospital for about a week --ready to admit myself.

Debbie played the piano since she was four. She practiced for an hour a day. At first, I didn't know whether I could stand it, but it was not long until the banging began to sound like a tune. We enjoyed her recitals, playing at church and on our radio broadcast. She graduated with honors from Rule High, then went on to marry High School sweetheart Bill Godfrey. They have two beautiful daughters who have started their own families. Debbie graduated in business from the University of Tennessee and worked in medical marketing for over 20 years. She loves God and wants others to know Him personally.

Shelby Family 1952

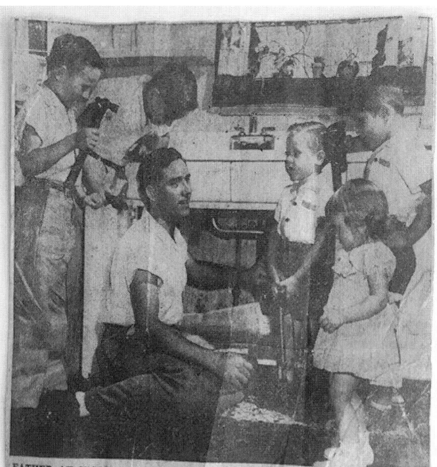

FATHER AT WORK—Today is Father's Day and families throughout the country will call attention to Dad's importance in the home by honoring him with gifts. Fathers will be the subject of praise in many ministers' sermons. Training the children is one of father's biggest responsibilities. The children of Wiley Shelby, 721 Virginia Avenue, gather around him to learn about fixing a pipe under the kitchen sink. Left to right are Charles, 7; George, 10; Stephen, 3; Gary, 5; and Debra, 19 months. The Shelby children can learn a lot about fixing leaky pipes from their father and Mrs. Shelby always rests assured the job will be done right when he sets about to do it. Shelby, 28 is a plumber.

Father's Day 1954

Mike has tinkered with things since he was small. He likes to see how things work or fix things that don't work. Once the youngster got his hands on a cigarette lighter. Before we knew it, his hands were badly burned and we were on our way to the hospital. He learned a valuable lesson as they put his hands in ice up to his elbows for several hours. I had a hard time keeping him still during this ordeal. Thank God, there were no visible scars.

He took apart and built everything from tape recorders to model cars. In middle school he was chess champ. In high school, he pursued Fulton High's electronics path, attended summer school and graduated early. He actively worked in the church, playing piano or organ and leading the singing. As expected, he met his wife Susan Wilson through church. Mike became a deacon, formed a quartet and owned his own automobile repair garage. Mike and Susan had a talented baby boy Shannon, but later divorced. As time passed, Mike married Gail Holmes and adopted her daughter Kari. Shannon and Kari started their own families and are contributing many beautiful grandchildren.

Mike and Gail formed a Gospel music group in 1989 that they called "Eternal Vision." They have traveled the US and abroad sharing the Gospel through testimony and song.

Mike was the baritone singer and also the owner, manager, and bus driver. Gail sang alto and tenor and was also chief financial officer, managed the schedule, and stocked the groceries on the bus. Their son Shannon plays every instrument you could ever think of, including keyboard, guitar, drums, and harmonica, even though he never had any lessons. He also writes most of the group's songs. Originally Gary was the fourth member of the group. When he retired they replaced him with Stuart Stallings, who is not related. Stuart sings base and is also the group's comedian.

I sang with the group for a short time. I still make occasional guest appearances.

Although Gail passed from a serious illness in 2015, their Eternal Vision ministry continues today. Mike is so talented he can play most any instrument, sings lead beautifully, and continues to witness for God. Mike has a recording studio and his group is widely known throughout the Southern Gospel circuit; from TV, radio concerts, and even cruise ship performances.

On various occasions, Imogene and I were fortunate to travel with them on their big Eagle bus from state to state, sharing the Gospel. We visited Laney Road Baptist Church in Jacksonville, where Pastor Wimberly invited me to preach. I remember many people came to the altar to be saved or rededicate their lives to God that weekend. I don't count or keep a record of those things but God does! And that's what really counts.

I am **eternally** grateful for the opportunities of serving our God with Eternal Vision!

http://www.eternalvision.net/

Dwayne will always be our baby boy. Every one of us pampered him from the time he was born. Dwayne is blessed as a musician and songwriter. His occupation is Heat & Air, but his heart is music.

One of the happiest times I remember was while he attended Beaumont Elementary School. Principal Dewey Lee awarded us with a signed plaque on April 27, 1976

"In grateful recognition of Mr. and Mrs. W.E. Shelby for their fine Christian influence on their children: George, Charles, Gary, Steve, Debbie, Mike and Dwayne. For their high ideals and exemplary conduct while students in this school. We pray for each the very best that life may have in store."

From his marriage to Debbie Watson, they have a son Brandon (also talented musician) and daughter Mandy (beauty, brains and talent), starting their families for the next generation. Dwayne later married Chasity Newsome and claims her daughters as his own. The Shelby clan continues to expand as God gives us precious gifts!

Carson Brewer, Knoxville New Sentinel Nov 2 1984

I made a ring out of a stainless steel nut. Each of my sons wore it until he married then passed it along to the next in line. After all the boys married, I had the ring mounted on a plaque for my daughter to display as a keepsake. The inscription reads: "Debbie The ring you weren't able to wear is now entrusted in your care. Love, Daddy"

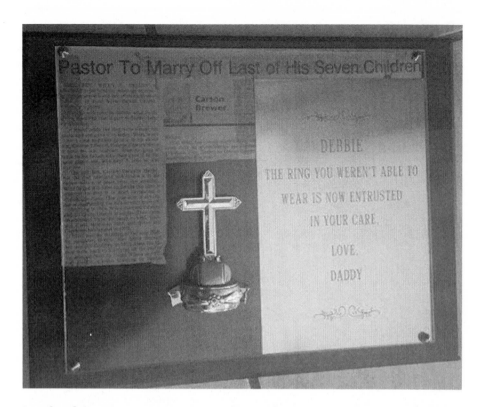

I asked Dwayne to write a song based on the idea of the California Gold Rush of 1849. Back then a lot of people rushed out to stake a claim if they found even a few little nuggets. They worked hard to find the big vein or "Mother Load" before someone else could find and claim it. Dwayne loves to sing and play gospel music. He has written several songs, so my request was not a surprise. He had a beautiful song in just a few hours. He said he was driving home from work and God gave it to him so fast that he had to stop at the roadside and write it down.

I stake my claim in the blood of Jesus.
Satan can't get it from me—though He tries to steal my nuggets.
The more I work and pray, the more and bigger my nuggets.
By Faith, one day I will get to walk the street of gold in heaven
        with my Savior.

And if I go and prepare a place for you, I will come again, and receive you unto myself; that where I am, there ye may be also. (John 14:3)

A time to keep and a time to cast away

A shoe salesman witnessed an incident of charity that restored his faith in people. One cold day in downtown Truro, Nova Scotia, the shoe salesman noticed a little boy standing outside in his bare feet on the hot air register, trying to keep warm. As he wondered what he should do, a lady approached the boy. After a few words with the barefoot boy, she brought him into the shoe store. She bought him new shoes and heavy woolen socks. He tried awkwardly to thank her and then asked, "Are you God's wife?" Taken aback by the question, she took her time replying. "No son, I'm just one of His children." He replied as he ran out the door, "Well, I knew you must be some kin to Him!"

On August 15, 1993, we celebrated our 50th wedding anniversary with about 125 people (family and friends)

at the Lion's Club facility in Fountain City Park. We had a wonderful evening of memories, gifts, and best wishes. Among the many treasured gifts, was a Proclamation Plaque from Mayor Victor Ashe.

*"...made on behalf of the people of the city of Knoxville, by his Honor the Mayor Victor Ashe, proclaiming the date to be **Rev. and Mrs. Wiley E. Shelby Day** in our city and urge all citizens to join in this observance."*

The proclamation noted the date of Aug 4, 1993 as our 50th anniversary and that congratulations should be extended to us. Further it listed what this union had produced up to that time: seven children, nineteen grandchildren, and ten great grandchildren.

Since I was retired at the time, I had taken time to look back at those years through my collection of cards, notes, and children's drawings. Many of these things, other people would have thrown away after a few days. Those were precious memories to me, so I put them in three different books: *50th Good Times Back*, *Patches of Joy*, and *Down Memory Lane from 1945-1993*. I spent many hours looking back on our married life and seeing how good God had been to us. These tell a story just as good as picture albums, or better! Pictures don't tell the whole story of how much you mean to the people in your life. Some people may incorrectly call these scrapbooks. Scrap is something you throw away. I call them treasure books. When I go to them I dig up all kinds of pleasure. Just think how good God has been to this "ole" country preacher. That's what I want to share with the world!

Whether it is a bought card from the store or a card made by a first-grader, it delivers fond memories. Many of the cards were from Sunday School children where I was their pastor. I may not even recognize them as grownups. But the joy of knowing that it meant something to them back then, certainly, meant much to me.

Forgive me. I had to stop writing to spend time looking at my memory books again. As I wipe away tears of joy, they bring back memories of wonderful times in my life. Times like bouncing my babies on my knee to the tune of "Trot a Little Horsey" or "Yankee Doodle." Special times after they started school, enjoying the papers they brought home to show their work or even helping them with home work!

The home we shared has a story in every corner. If walls could talk, I probably couldn't write it all down! Even after our children were grown, the home came alive again on Sundays after church. Lunch was always set, expecting a full house. Many generations of Shelby's made it a routine to come "home" on a regular basis. It was like Christmas, Thanksgiving, or Easter all year long. They knew Mom always has something good to eat on Sunday. Our stomachs were filled and our home was filled with children, grandchildren, and often great-grandchildren.

Imogene may not have known how to cook when we got married, but she got plenty of experience over the years. She loved to spread the **tables**. There were so many of us that we had two dining room tables, a kitchenette table, and space for the kids in the living room if they wanted to watch TV. It was not only about the food. The fellowship our family shared far exceeded the value of the food.

Of course, I helped Mamaw (Imogene) more and more in the kitchen as we aged. I guess I got in her way more than I helped at times. I followed her around trying to share some of her work, like cleanup duties as we cooked (washing/drying dishes, pots, and pans). One thing I won't do is get up at four o'clock Sunday morning to put the roast or ham in the oven to bake. That sounds like something she would like to do, so I would say go for it.

At Thanksgiving and Christmas, she depended on me to do the fruitcakes and stuff the turkey. The fruitcakes were made a few days before, but the turkey would be stuffed the night before and baked all night long. That is when I did my night cooking. We expected the children, with their families, to start arriving about 7 AM.

There is nothing like a house filled with smells of turkey, dressing, and goodies on Christmas morning! We started eating as soon as the sausage balls and coffee were ready. Then we gathered in the living room to open presents. The youngest go first so they can play with their new toy. Since I am the oldest, that makes me last to open presents; and that is usually about 12 PM or 1 PM. After all the presents, wrapping paper, and boxes were cleaned up, we put lunch on the table.

Sounds like a mad house, but everyone tried to help—even if that meant to step out in the yard waiting for a clear path to the tables. Usually, we had thirty to forty people (or more) for lunches in this little house. Often, friends and playmates showed up and were welcomed as family here too.

The sad or quiet time came after everyone left. Imogene and I could finally see presents that our children had given us. By 7 PM, we would reset supper for a smaller group. Debbie's family and Dwayne's family usually came back to share more goodies and reminisce about the day's events.

It didn't take a lot of money. It came about with the love, joy, and fun of our family. My prayer is that our family will always be close knit, continue to get along, and share their love and time with one another; as I believe God meant it to be. Each of us will have to do his or her part to make it continue as one big happy family. I also believe God has blessed us **because** we are a Christian family.

Chapter 5. NOT THE END

A time to get and a time to lose

Nov 26, 2013

I write this while waiting for Imogene to come off the dialysis machine. The last four years have been difficult. In 2009, my wife Imogene suddenly got sick (congestive heart failure, heart attack, kidney failure, etc…). She also took some serious falls. We were at the hospital several times. I just couldn't get started back writing, even sitting here at dialysis for four hours three times a week. I couldn't think of anything else except taking care of her and doing the work she had been doing: cooking, washing, house cleaning. I don't know how she kept up with all that and took care of seven children and me! And as a pastor's wife, she had a lot on her. If the children had not helped out and been such good kids we probably wouldn't have made it for all these years. God gave us the most wonderful family of six boys and one girl. They all accepted the Lord at a young age and God still uses them and they still help mom and dad in our old days for there is so much that we can't do now. Thank God for our family.

I look back to our 65th Wedding Anniversary celebration at Cloudland State Park in Georgia. Debbie, our daughter, drove us to a surprise destination. We didn't know where we were going until she stopped at a grocery store and there we met our son George and his wife Gladys. That's when we figured out it wasn't just a joy ride. When we arrived at the campground, there were four cabins full of the Shelby clan! The next day, more of the

Shelby family showed up. There were 96 of our loved ones there if I counted correctly! We had cookouts, played games, talked of old times, sang together, laughed together and just had a wonderful time at the beautiful park.

Our 70th Wedding Anniversary celebration was at Fountain City Park in Knoxville. Again, a crowd of over a hundred Shelby's and friends celebrated with us. There were a lot of photos, food, preparation and a wonderful party. We even met some great-great grandchildren for the first time.

She lying alone in a cold dark room.
Not a friend or loved one there
waiting & listening for a soft hello
But she has No one who cares.

But then she thinks oh I have a friend
A friend who really cares
He's Here right now to take me home
He's My Jesus And His Home I'll share.

That Night God came & took her home
No more lonely days or nights
She right there with Jesus happy &
loved.
In a home in a land so beautiful
& Bright.
So no more lonely Cold dark room
Lonesome sad or Blue
She gone where loved ones
friends and love
In heaven where all things
are new

Imogene's handwriting found on the back of a 2004 church program:

At some time in our lives, all of us must face up to the reality of death. The loss of a loved one is one of the most difficult and challenging human experiences. Each of us has to come to terms with the loss in our own way. But, when the loved one is a child of God, they are going to a better place. "The Lord giveth and the Lord taketh away, Blessed be the name of the Lord." For she said, "I'm going home. I'm going home and it will be all right." I said, "Honey, we have been together for 70 years. Wait a little longer." She waited a few hours and said, "I'll wait on you." I said, "What?" She repeated, "I'll wait on you." I asked, "Where?" She answered, "Down on Hallelujah Avenue." I asked, "Is that like the Golden Street?" She replied, "Yes." Praise the Lord, I will see her once again some day.

Many friends and neighbors came by and sent encouraging words after my wife's passing. One particular six-page letter from our neighbors, Emma and George Tate meant so much to our family. Written, giving full glory to God, but filled with so much love and compassion. This is what God can do with you if you fully surrender yourself, present your body a living sacrifice and be not conformed to this world but be **transformed** by the renewing of your mind.

At the hospital, our nephew Alan Galloway sat with us, sang with us, prayed with us until the end. This is his witness delivered at the funeral:

"The love of a family can extend life. Maybe for just a few days, but I believe this from watching family the last three days. I watched the children, grandchildren and friends sitting beside the bedside of a loved one that was given four to five hours to live on Friday. I saw them take turns sitting one on each side of the bed holding her hand and not one time was she ever left alone. She was talked to and cried with and sang to and told over and over how much she was loved. And although I can't remember if it was Sunday morning or Monday morning ... I watched this Saint of God when everything medical showed the end should have already happened, I watched her breathing increase instead of going down the way it should have. There are many reasons why **they** think Aunt Imogene held on longer, but watching this family and friends over the last few days it becomes clear to me there was just one reason, she was not ready to leave the love of a family."

Funeral Tribute to Mamaw given by Shannon Shelby:

For those of you who may not know me, my name is Shannon Shelby. I am Mike Shelby's son and Imogene is my Mamaw. First of all I want to praise God for allowing me to be a part of this family. For blessing me with these godly grandparents who have helped mold me into who I am today—who have shown me the love of God through the lives that they have lived. What an incredible example! Not only an example of what Christ would have us to be; but, an amazing example of what God intended a marriage to be. Nearly 71 years of marriage! Let me ask you a question. How many of you are related to Mamaw in some form or another? Wow! What a legacy!

There is a popular decorative plaque and picture frame that's out now. Above where the picture goes, it says, 'All because two people fell in love.' That has never been more applicable than it is today. Nearly all of us are here simply because these two people fell in love. Because God in his infinite wisdom, put these two people together. Thank you for that, Lord. God has used them together as one, to touch lives for nearly three quarters of a century. Praise the Lord!

For me personally, they have literally always been there. God has blessed me with wonderful parents who have always been there as well, but the other constant in my life, has been my Mamaw and Papaw, literally since the hour that I was born. Every milestone in my life, major or minor, they have been there: every school function, choir recital, Kindergarten graduation, my baptism, eighth grade dance, graduation, prom, my wedding, and the birth of my daughter—their great granddaughter, etc...

And I know it has been the same for a lot of us. Most of us! Mamaw has stood for something her entire life. Something that she instilled within everyone she was ever around—something that I want to carry on—something that each of us **should** carry on: LOVE! Mamaw stood for and exemplified love, a direct reflection of the love that Christ has for us. And I praise God for her. For allowing this world to be a better, brighter place, just by having her in it. And boy, I'm gonna miss her. WE are going to miss her. But I believe she has reached her great reward!! And I've never known anyone that should have more jewels in their crown than Mamaw. Praise the Lord! I pray the people see her through us; that we love the way that she loved--The way that Jesus Loves!

There is a song that reminds me so much of Mamaw and Papaw by David Phelps, called "Legacy of Love." In the final bridge, it says, "Life is far too short, not to finally realize, that its long enough to make a difference in someone's life. Thank you Mamaw—Thank you for making a difference in my life. Thank you for making a difference in ALL of our lives. Thank you God for

Mamaw, for we know it was You working through her the entire time, and she would want You to get all of the Honor and Glory. And for that we praise You Lord! We are so grateful for Your Love!

Now most of us who have been around Mamaw for any length of time, especially when Papaw was preaching (and he got a little long-winded), knows that sometimes she could get a little impatient. Whenever that would happen, she did a little hand movement that became synonymous with Mamaw—the majority of us have seen it countless times. Well Mamaw, I love you ... I miss you ... and I'll see you real soon. So until then, while we all wait ... (does the thumb twirls like Mamaw to wrap it up.)

A PROCLAMATION
On Behalf Of The People Of
KNOX COUNTY
By His Honor The Mayor
Tim Burchett
To Publicly Recognize

Wiley & Imogene Shelby's 70th ANNIVERSARY

Whereas; On AUGUST 4, 1943 Wiley Edward Shelby & Imogene Charlotte Johnson were married in Knoxville; and

Whereas; With Imogene by his side Wiley served as cook in the army; and

Whereas; Over the years, they ministered through membership in several local churches while Wiley worked as a plumber and preached the Gospel; and

Whereas; Together they raised 7 above-average offspring, who produced 21 great grandchildren, 27 great-great grandchildren, 6 great-great-great and still counting; and

Whereas;

As a supportive wife, Imogene gets special recognition for putting up with Wiley for 70 years; and they both are granted showers of blessings for their future...

NOW, THEREFORE, I, MAYOR TIM BURCHETT, KNOX COUNTY MAYOR do hereby proclaim August 4, 2013 as

Wiley & Imogene Shelby Day

In Knox County, and urge all citizens to join in this observance.

The Virtuous Wife
Proverbs 31:10-31

10 Who can find a virtuous wife? For her worth is far above rubies.

11 The heart of her husband safely trusts her; So he will have no lack of gain.

12 She does him good and not evil All the days of her life.

13 She seeks wool and flax, And willingly works with her hands.

14 She is like the merchant ships, She brings her food from afar.

15 She also rises while it is yet night, And provides food for her household, And a portion for her maidservants.

16 She considers a field and buys it; From her profits she plants a vineyard.

17 She girds herself with strength, And strengthens her arms.

18 She perceives that her merchandise is good, And her lamp does not go out by night.

19 She stretches out her hands to the distaff, And her hand holds the spindle.

20 She extends her hand to the poor, Yes, she reaches out her hands to the needy.

21 She is not afraid of snow for her household, For all her household is clothed with scarlet.

22 She makes tapestry for herself; Her clothing is fine linen and purple.

23 Her husband is known in the gates, When he sits among the elders of the land.

24 She makes linen garments and sells them, And supplies sashes for the merchants.

25 Strength and honor are her clothing; She shall rejoice in time to come.

26 She opens her mouth with wisdom, And on her tongue is the law of kindness.

27 She watches over the ways of her household, And does not eat the bread of idleness.

28 Her children rise up and call her blessed; Her husband also, and he praises her:

29 "Many daughters have done well, But you excel them all."

30 Charm is deceitful and beauty is passing, But a woman who fears the Lord, she shall be praised.

31 Give her of the fruit of her hands, And let her own works praise her in the gates.

Imogene Charlotte Shelby

March 15, 1927 – March 24, 2014

Shelby, Imogene Charlotte, age 87 of Knoxville entered into eternal life, Monday, March 24, 2014. She leaves a legacy of love to five generations. Imogene was a loving and devoted wife, mother, sister, grandmother, great-grandmother, great-great-grandmother, and great-great-great-grandmother. She was a longtime member of Westside Baptist Church. Devoted to the Christian faith, she was instrumental in Bible Schools, Christmas plays and serving as a minister's wife. Imogene is survived by her loving husband, Reverend Wiley E. Shelby; sons and daughters-in-law, George and Gladys Shelby, Charles and Faye Shelby, Gary and Beckie Shelby, Steve and Charlotte Shelby, Michael and Gail Shelby and Dwayne and Chasity Shelby; daughter Debbie Godfrey; grandchildren Tony and Denise Shelby, Connie Strickland, Dennis and Spring Shelby, Kimm Bell, Mark and Elizabeth Shelby, Melissa Shelby, Kevin and Sarah Shelby, Karen Shelby Gillespie, Lynn and Sue Shelby, Robert Shelby, Christopher and Lisa Shelby, Stephanie and Keith Owensby, Jennifer and Ricky Henry, Julie and Cat Petrey, Jessica Raxter, Scott and Missy Campbell, Shannon and Kayla Shelby, Kari and Nathan Calfee, Brandon and Tiffany Shelby and Mandy Shelby; great-grandchildren, great-great-grandchildren, and great-great-great-grandchildren too numerous to count; brother and sister-in-law, Bill and Sue Johnson; several nieces, nephews, friends and loved ones; and special four-legged companion Buddy. A celebration of Imogene's life will be held 7:00 PM Wednesday at Rose Mortuary Broadway Chapel with Reverend Ronnie Dobson,

Reverend Josh Greene, and Reverend David Knight officiating. Family and friends will meet 11:00 AM Thursday at Highland South Memorial Gardens for interment services. The family would like to extend a very special thank you to the Doctors, staff and caregivers during Imogene's illness. In lieu of flowers, memorials may be made to the church or charity of your choice. Online condolences may be sent to www.rosemortuary.com. The family will receive friends from 5:00 PM to 7:00 PM Wednesday at Rose Mortuary Broadway Chapel.

And Jabez called on the God of Israel, saying, Oh that thou wouldest bless me indeed, and enlarge my coast, and that thine hand might be with me, and that thou wouldest keep me from evil, that it may not grieve me! And God granted him that which he requested. (1 Chronicles 4:10)

About twenty years after I stopped pastoring Elm Street Church, I wasn't getting many calls to preach. Knowing I still had work to do for the Lord, I prayed the Jabez Prayer. Not long after that is when I began taking Imogene to dialysis. For five years, Monday, Wednesday, Friday, four hours per day I sat in the waiting room with other family members. We often enjoyed a good Bible discussion and I had several opportunities to witness for my God. On July 10, 2012, Imogene's doctors added physical therapy treatment for swelling of Breast Lymph Nodes. With therapy, we met a wonderful Christian, Amy White at Benchmark. We talked about the Lord, His goodness, and our families for about 18 months. My borders were being extended to witness outside of the pulpit.

A day or two before Imogene's death, I recall talking to God. God spoke to me directly about my future. He said, "After she passes away, you will be going on the bus with Eternal Vision to minister to others." Needless to say, it was no surprise when Mike came to me after her passing, "Daddy, you are going with us on the bus." While traveling with them, I only missed two EV appointments: once I had a preaching appointment (without EV singers) and once I was in the hospital.

Four months later, I told Mike, "I have something to tell you." He asked, "What is it, Dad?" "Remember when you told me I was going to start going with you on the Eternal Vision Bus? I knew that because God had told me, when we were talking a few days back. He must have been talking to you, too." He shook his head. On January 16 we had services in a bar in Virginia! Saturday night, January 17, we had a good church service with a full house and several people coming down to the altar. Sunday morning, January 18, another wonderful service in a different church, people standing in the back. At Altar Call, the pastor and I prayed with so many people, they just kept coming. After the service closed, I ate lunch with the group then went to sit on the bus—just the Lord and me. All at once I heard a voice (I don't know if it was out loud or just in my head). He said, "See I answered your prayer. You prayed the Jabez Prayer for your borders to be extended. I have extended your borders and I am going to enlarge them even more." Praise God! I had to shout a little, for I had forgotten that I prayed that prayer.

While traveling on the bus, Preacher Ron Dotson of Anchor Holds Baptist called, wanting me to preach that Sunday morning. When I told him where I was he said we will just have to get together some other time.

My first cruise with Eternal Vision was on the Carnival Liberty on Feb 8, 2015. We got on board at 12 noon, left Port Canaveral at 4 PM. Boy did I ever stuff myself for the next 14 days. I could eat anytime and ice cream in between! — I think I spent more time eating than anything else.

Everyone was so nice to me on the cruise. Even Mike paid extra just so I could have a cabin to myself with a King size bed! He may have thought I would spend more time in my cabin since I am over 88 years old. But not so! I love to see all I can and there was too much going on. Cabin Number 8338 just wasn't large enough to hold me. Besides, I spent too much time alone at home. When I did go out on the ship I admit I would sometimes get turned around. But most of the time, I had someone with me to point me in the right direction. All the folks in our group took care of me like family. Mike was busy taking care of Gail as her health declined; she was in a wheelchair.

Each night we ate in the Silver Dining room on the 4th deck at 8:15 PM. We could order anything we wanted from the menu; and I did! The rest of the day we could eat at other food counters, restaurants or grills all day long!

One particular night at dinner, there was music playing and everyone was laughing, talking, and having a great time. Stewart Stalling's family sat behind me at the next table. He had left the table to prepare for the next Eternal Vision show but his two daughters (ages 24 and 28) started kidding me. Like most everyone there, they called me "Papaw". They said "Papaw, Daddy told us not to let any of those boys on the ship kiss us on the cheek." I joined in the lighthearted fun and kissed them on the cheek. Then they wanted to dance with me between the tables. There was hardly enough room to walk much less dance. It was all in good clean fun and seemed like everyone there was having a good time.

Our first stop was the Island of Grand Turk, a beautiful little island! There were plenty of souvenir stands, but most of them too costly for my pocket book. T-shirts, watches, diamonds, jewelry of all kinds, but I had no one to buy them for. Salt & pepper shakers, but Imogene doesn't collect them anymore. She left hundreds of them with me when she went home to be with Jesus. You wonder how I know she is there? She left a wonderful testimony. She told me she was going home and it will be all right. Later she told me she would wait for me down on Hallelujah Avenue. Praise God. I believe she will be waiting for me when God calls me home.

On this Island I saw the space capsule, space suit and rocket exhibit. Mike was with me showing me around since he had been there before. We met two very nice women from England that were on the ship docked next to ours. Mike snapped a picture of us. Then back to the ship.

A storm came up so we stayed tied to the dock at Grand Turk. The ship bounced around and rocked side to side. About 10 PM, Mother Nature decided to cooperate with us and winds calmed sufficiently for us to safely sail to our next port. Due to the weather delay, we were forced to cancel our visit to San Juan. So the next day we had Fun at Sea, and then headed to St. Maarten for our next scheduled visit. (Captain Leonardo Contirino said we would be automatically refunded the $17.72 for taxes, fees and port expense since we didn't see San Juan.) St. Maarten had beautiful mountains on the Island and the port we visited was so nice! The ocean was clear blue unlike the pretty green ocean at Grand Turk.

Eternal Vision sang each night. Up until the last two nights, I sat in the audience. Then, Paul Roark the cruise organizer/MC called me up to the desk where he was directing the program. Roark said, "We don't usually do this but you have been such a good supporter for us that we are going to let you sing on stage tonight!" So I sang **The Old Ship of Zion**, with backup singers Mike Shelby, Shane Roark and Stewart Stalling. We got a standing ovation! So the next night we sang, **My Real Home**. That was the last evening for EV to sing on the cruise so I say God did extend my borders out into the ocean! I thanked God for answering my prayers. Be sure you want what you ask for—you just might get it. For My God will answer in His own way and His own time—Matthew 21:22. And all things, whatsoever ye shall ask in prayer, believing, ye shall receive.

Sunday morning, February 15, 2015 we disembarked from the ship at Port Canaveral. As usual, one of the bags was lost for a while. We loaded the bus and my thoughts were to express my thanks to the captain and crew. I enjoyed the cruise aboard the beautiful Carnival Liberty. I was delighted to sail on this ship. I agree that the ship team worked very hard to provide us with warm and friendly service; from the stateroom steward who turned down the bed and left us clean towels, animal surprises, etc., to the dining room waiters who remembered my preference night after night. It left me smiling with delight and a memorable fun-filled vacation. The service was second to none! I wanted to tell the Captain how his team was responsible for insuring my needs were met and the care of my return home was a fun and memorable first cruise. I never did get to do that.

When we left St. Maarten, it was short-sleeve weather. But back on the bus, as we drove toward home, stopped for Arby's, ate on the bus, and returned to Knoxville about 11 PM, I was ready to go back! By Monday morning we had snow and ice lasting until Sunday Feb 22. The temperature got as low as 4 degrees but I got plenty of rest. I had been in the house too long.

At 88 years old, I came home with happy wonderful memories of my first cruise. I did not get seasick. And, I got to exercise my faith in the Lord Jesus Christ, beyond the border of our great nation with Eternal Vision Ministries and many friends who went with us.

HE HATH MADE EVERYTHING BEAUTIFUL IN HIS TIME

A time to embrace

He hath made everything beautiful in His time: also he hath set the world in their heart, so that no man can find out the work that God maketh from the beginning to the end. (Ecclesiastes 3:11)

Ruth, Cruise, Florida Ministry

God is in the details! At Christmas in the Smokies, November 2015, I set up the tapes and CD's for sale by Eternal Vision in an exhibit booth in the lobby. I am the Dad to them and have been traveling with the group since Imogene's death. Every year, my friends Tom and

Sandra Turner came to hear the concerts. They said they weren't coming this year but others from their church, CrossBridge Church in Madeira Beach, Florida, wanted to come so they came also. This year was different. Sandra had asked her mom, Ruth Johansen from North Carolina to come with them.

Ruth was rooming with Brenda Brown, the EV group's booking agent. Brenda introduced us the first night as they came into the lobby. I asked Ruth if she wanted to sit with me to sell tapes. She said she would!

As we talked, I asked her where she put God in her life. She held both hands up and replied, "At the top of my life!" "Me, too." I replied, "Let's talk some more..."

We talked about our lives. Her husband died in 2012, my wife died in 2014. We just seemed to click. When we could get a break from the sales table, we walked around the parking lot to learn more about each other. I wanted to show her the EV traveling bus but it was locked. I talked about being a pastor and learned she had taught many years of Sunday School.

Ruth grew up in New York, had lived many years in Virginia then moved to North Carolina with her son and his wife after her husband died. Of course, I told her I was born in Knoxville and stayed there. She had given birth to five kids, 3 boys and 2 girls. One baby died, and they adopted two kids. I learned a lot more about her with her quick Yankee talk. My southern drawl is much slower so she still had a lot more to learn about me. Then we went in to hear the concert and eat dinner.

My son Mike (not Ruth's son Mike), came to our table to ask, "Where have you been? I have been looking for you and got worried because you are always sitting at the exhibit table." I told him that Ruth and I had been just walking around. He just stared at me.

Ruth and I spent three and one-half hours together that first day. We said 'goodnight' after dinner. She went to her room and I returned to my home in Knoxville for the night. The second night, we met in the lobby at the exhibit table. Mike stared at us and walked past several times. But when we could get a break, we walked outside again. After a few minutes of listening more to her, I found out she was a good Christian woman. The night before, I had thought about how I might want this woman in my life because it seemed God had placed her there beside me. I got the nerve and asked her, "What would you think if I asked you to marry me?" She said, "Oh, I don't know about that..." We went into the concert. Ruth sat with her daughter Sandra and Tom her son-in-law. I sat across the room with Brenda Brown, EV's agent.

After the concert, Ruth and I talked for a few minutes. I did get a goodnight kiss and boy that felt good! Then the third night, we shared a good time, a goodnight kiss, and a promise to call each other after we returned to our homes.

Ruth had a large walk-in closet at her son's house. When I called her or she called me, she said she would go into the closet and sit on the stool as we talked for an hour or more. Her son, Michael said we were acting like teenagers (but I was 89 and she was 83). It was fun and I was very lonely! She filled the gap.

I asked Ruth to come for Christmas dinner but she said she wasn't good with a bunch of strangers. She asked, "What about the day after Christmas?" I said, "Yes, yes, yes!"

She left her home in North Carolina about 5 AM and got to my house about 9 AM. We had a wonderful time together, walking my dog Buddy in the park and learning more about each other. When we returned to my home I cooked her a fine dinner including fried chicken and fried okra and zucchini (which she had never eaten before.) She said she loved it but she may have been trying to butter me up. I showed her all my plants in my yard, enjoying walking again.

That evening I was leaving again to travel with Eternal Vision. Ruth was traveling to Florida to visit with Sandra and Tom. When the bus arrived, I told Mike and the group what a great Christian person she was and how much I cared for her. We went on to the concert but I kept thinking about Ruth and how much I wanted her in my life.

I wanted to ask Ruth to marry me. I was going with Eternal Vision on a gospel cruise in February and wanted to take Ruth on the cruise for our honeymoon! I called her while she was still in Florida. She was visiting with the EV agent, Brenda Brown at the time. "Are you sitting down?" I asked. She replied, "Yes..." "Is Brenda sitting down, too?" I asked. "Yes..." She answered. "Then turn the speaker on the phone up loud so you can hear me." I said. "Ok..." "Will you marry me?" I blurted out. She yelled, "Yes!" In the background, I heard Brenda laughing and clapping.

A few days later, I was on the EV bus as we headed to the next concert. Mike was sitting at the steering wheel. I blurted out that I was going to get married. He sat there dazed for a few seconds then said, "Daddy, if that's what it takes to make you happy, it will be alright with me... just don't bring in five or six kids for me to raise!" I laughed, "I'm not Abraham, you know." He smiled and said, "And she is not Sarah." All the guys on the bus were having a good laugh about this.

Another few days passed. I told my son Charles that I was planning to marry Ruth. He was concerned that I had only known her for a short time. "Dad, don't you think you ought to wait until you know more about her?" I replied, "No son, I'm nearly ninety years old! I don't have much time to wait." He dropped his head and said, "That will be okay by me if that will make you happy. "

January 1, 2016, Mike's wife Gail Shelby died, after suffering a long illness. Ruth wanted to attend the funeral, so she drove up from Florida to stay at my daughter Debbie's home. When she arrived that afternoon, we talked about Gail's illness, the funeral and our wedding plans. The date was set for January 27, 2016.

So many people came to Gail's funeral. She was well known and well-loved from years in the EV ministry. Also, Gail had worked with the Mull Singing Convention on television and other southern Gospel radio programs.

I introduced Ruth as my fiancé to those attending the funeral. Many people came up to us to congratulate us on the announcement. Two ladies said that if they knew I wanted to get married, they would have spent more time flirting with me. I told Ruth, "I hope you're not the jealous type." She replied, "They can hug you all they want so long as they know that you are mine."

From Knoxville, Ruth went back to North Carolina where she lived with her son Michael and his wife Cyndi. Wedding plans took shape. Michael would walk his mom down the aisle. Ruth's daughter Sandra Turner, the co-pastor at CrossBridge Church in Florida, would officiate. Ruth's daughter Cassandra Stetson would be her maid of honor. My daughter Debbie and my granddaughter Melissa Shelby would plan the reception. My son, George would be my best man. The wedding was at the Fountain City Lion's Club and well attended by friends and family.

Shannon sang "Love Me Tender" as Ruth walked down the aisle. She was beautiful! I was excited to have her as my wife. As officiating minister, Sandra used the old fashion wedding vows of love, honor, and obey; she did a great job. There were three jars of sand placed in front of us to remind us that our lives were being co-mingled. Ruth and I poured our sand containers together to become one with God, just like the intermingling sand. Then Ruth's daughter-in-law Cyndi sang a beautiful song and we were pronounced "Husband and Wife". We ate bar-b-que with all the fixin's and wedding cake, my grandson Chris and his wife Lisa took many professional pictures, then my son Dwayne and his wife Chasity sang, followed by several other singers and well-wishers at the reception. Our families pitched in to make sure every detail was covered for a perfect day. Afterwards, Ruth's family came back to our house to get acquainted. Ruth added six wonderful step-children to my family— Michael, Patrick, Sandra, Mark, Dennis, and Cassandra— and spouses and more grandchildren and great-grandchildren.

The first week of February we were off on our honeymoon cruise out of Tampa— along with Eternal Vision and their entourage of followers. We listened to great music, ate great food, walked around the ship, ate again, got off at different ports, ate again... you get the idea? What a honeymoon!

Soon after returning home, Pastor Rick from CrossBridge, Sandra's church in Madeira Beach, called to ask if I would consider  moving to Florida and assuming the role of pastoral care at the church. He got to know me through Eternal Vision's concerts. I told Pastor Rick that Ruth had to help me in all that I did through the church. He agreed. After much prayer, Ruth and I decided to try it for one month. We brought some things with us for the month of March. We decided this is where God wanted us.

Our job was to visit the sick and elderly of the CrossBridge Church. We also prayed with people on the phone, passed out lots of tracts, and participated in church events. The church people seemed to love having us there in ministry. We had a nice set-up living with Sandra and Tom in St. Pete. We had our own entrance, bedroom, living room and bath. We shared their kitchen but we all got along, even the three dogs.

I even got to fish some in Florida but of course never enough. On one occasion, Sandra and Tom went fishing with us. I caught a three-inch fish. Sandra took a photo but thought it would be funny to make it look like a whopper. She made it look at least 18 inches long; then she sent it to my daughter in Knoxville. Debbie immediately put it on Facebook for all to see before I could tell her the real size of the fish. We all got a big laugh over that.

Sandra received a call from Annie Johnson, the Coordinator of Palm Gardens Nursing Home. Annie asked if Crossbridge had anyone who could come to preach for their residents every other month. When Sandra told me

I said, "Yes, praise the LORD! I love to preach God's Word to everyone." So now I also serve at Palm Gardens. Annie gives me free reign to conduct a service for an hour. The residents seem to love it. They pick out songs I love to sing that always have a message about the LORD. Ruth comes with me to shake hands with each patient and listen and show them we care.

Another assisted living facility called but was much different. She required a full background of information on me: where was I born, where I attended school, years preaching, etc. I told her I have preached over 55 years, on the radio for 16 years, and pastored four churches. She restricted me to 20 minutes and no need for me to sing since they had singers. She also instructed me **not** to preach on "how to be saved" because they were already saved. So, I preached on "The Homecoming in Heaven."

I started the message in Genesis about Adam's sin that brought sin down on all mankind; we are all sinners. Followed by, to get ready for the Homecoming in Heaven, we must be born again. God had to give His Son to pay the sin debt that we could not pay. In order to go to Heaven, we have to know that we are sinners, and believe that Jesus died for our sins and rose again from the dead. We must believe that Jesus is the only way to be saved from eternity in hell. We must ask Him to forgive us our sins, make a complete turn around, and serve Him.

Everyone loved the sermon. One man commented, "You really made it plain how to be saved." I even sang "My Real Home." With Ruth by my side, we continue to do what God has called us to do, "Preach, pray and visit with the sick in the hospitals and in homes."

Happy First Anniversary Cruise Feb 2017

Part II: Mark's Story

... also he hath set the world in their heart, so that no man can find out the work that God maketh from the beginning to the end. (Ecclesiastes 3:11)

My grandchildren, no doubt will carry on the love of God into future generations! I am so proud of each of them. All have survived difficult times with the help of God. Below is just one example that assures me and I hope it will bless the readers as well.

Read this story in his own words, as Charles's son, Mark Shelby, gave it to me.

God makes it very clear in scripture that we are to look after the less fortunate. We are to comfort the sick and the afflicted. When we do this we are very close to His heart because they are always very close to His heart. And when we serve them, we are also serving Him in a very real way.

I think I had been guilty of living a very "Americanized" version of Christianity. One that says, if you are suffering, it is your responsibility to try to pick yourself up. After all, every good Christian quotes the verse, "God helps those who help themselves", right? There's a big problem with that thought. It is not in the Bible, and it is NOT the heart of God. God's design is specifically for us to suffer and have need so that we can turn to Him and allow Him to get the credit when He meets our needs.

I remember specific conversations with elderly Christians who were going through a serious illness. More than once I'd hear them say how they were just so tired, and ready to go home if the Lord was ready to take them. And I recall thinking to myself "No! You are never supposed to give up like that! How could you love life so little that you'd just give up?" Well I don't think that anymore.

Boy, did I have a lot to learn! But like so many of us know all too well, when God is ready to teach you something, He has no problem getting your attention! I was getting ready to be taught a real lesson. I didn't know it then but I was getting ready to get a PhD in suffering and humility. And you know what? I can honestly say today that I thank God that He loves me enough to prune away the bad branches and dead areas of my spiritual self.

I can't tell you how difficult this has been just to write 'my story' down. In some ways, writing it forces me to relive it in a way that I'd never really want to do. But in the late winter of 2010, as is often the case, I was about to come to see the worst in myself, and discover the best in a Loving God who suffered more than we could ever know so that one day we might be made like Him!

I guess it's fair to say that God allowed me to get sick. Really sick. In fact, I spent nine or ten weeks in the hospital, flat on my back, and then another four weeks at home, again, flat on my back, staring at the ceiling... That's ninety-eight days, or two thousand three hundred and fifty-two hours! That's one hundred and forty-one thousand, one hundred and twenty minutes... Well, you get the picture. And you know what? When something like that happens to you, you have plenty of time to sit and think. You can only count the ceiling tiles just so many times before you begin to analyze your life. To try and make some sense out of things. "Poor, poor ME! How did it ever come to this?!!"

I don't want to get too far ahead of my own story, but I can tell you that there were plenty of dark hours during that time. And more than once I can remember crying out to God that it was all just too much, knowing that I couldn't take much more. I can remember thinking that I was just so tired that if He'd only take me I'd be more than ready to go. When that thought creeps in, and you know it is true, it is a very sobering thing. Still, God in His mercy always seemed to provide someone to come along and lift me back up.

Satan often comes to us at our darkest hours and lowest times, seeking to destroy our will and rob us of our peace in Christ. I had made up my mind that I was never going to let anyone see just how bad my pain and suffering was if I could help it. I made a real effort to be as upbeat and positive as possible. But he often got to me and planted seeds of doubt and fear. And at the risk of sounding like a big baby, I have to be truthful and admit that there were a lot of tears shed through my own darkest days.

During one such time my mother and I chatted on the phone for a few minutes. As any mother could, she sensed something was really wrong. I don't know why but at that moment I just burst into tears. I told her I was so tired and that I didn't know how much more I could take. She and I must have cried together for twenty minutes that afternoon. And yet, somehow, I felt better. Thank you, God, for a mother's heart and intuition!

On a second such occasion things seemed darker still. But I think the conversation I had that day with my Papaw helped me to turn a corner in a very real sense. On that particular evening I was really struggling. I was in so much pain and it was all I could do to try my best to hide it. I tried hard to smile for visitors that came to see me. I was upbeat with the doctors, nurses and tech staff that attended to me. In all ways, I was the perfect example of a "good patient."

But deep inside, I was struggling mightily. Maybe even with God. I wasn't angry with Him. I never blamed Him. But it seemed that in an instant everything in my life that I had taken for granted was being ripped away from me. I was scared. I was confused. I was hurting and I was just really tired. So I put in the call to my Papaw Wiley and Mamaw Imogene.

I tried my best to sound cheerful and upbeat but I'm sure now that God had prepared Papaw that day with a special measure of insight, discernment and wisdom. In my best upbeat voice I did my best to sound cheerful but don't think I'd said a full sentence when there was just silence on the other end, then came the words I can still hear to this day. "What's wrong, son?"

It was as if in that moment every wall I'd carefully erected came tumbling down. I was a forty-year-old man, yet he still called me "son." I was his grandson, yet he called me, "son." I had so much to **fix** in my own life, yet my Papaw still considered me a "son." I could hear the tears and compassion in his own voice.

I let go of everything. I remember telling him that I was just too tired and that I didn't know if I could go on much longer. I told him how I'd made a deal with myself to be the most upbeat and positive patient possible. I told him that I was grateful to be alive, but that I was scared for my health, my family and my future. I explained that I was in so much pain, yet there was nothing that could be done medically to stop it. I told him that I just had to lay there and suffer, and I didn't really know how much more I could take. I don't remember a lot of what he told me, but what he did best was just cry with me and he kept saying, "That's alright son, tell it to God. He wants you to and He understands."

We talked for a while. He and I talked about God's purpose in the mystery of suffering. He didn't try to explain it away or trivialize it. But he did assure me that God was capable of seeing me through it and that when I did come through the other side I would look upon it as one of the pivotal experiences of my Christian journey.

He did ask me to promise God that when I was healed that I would tell others my testimony so that God could get the glory He rightfully deserved. At the time I didn't see how God could possibly get glory from my messed up experience. But since then I have tried to be faithful to that calling.

Papaw assured me that he and Mamaw would continue praying for me day and night. And I felt comforted by that. I can tell you first hand that as a Christian when you are facing the darkest hours and toughest times you'll really be able to sense the comfort of the Holy Spirit in the moments when others are praying for you. I knew specifically when others were lifting me up in prayer. It was tangible and very real to me.

So in a very real sense it is because of the encouragement from my Papaw that I am finally writing this testimony down. But it isn't an easy thing to do. It is truly my prayer that God will use some part of my story to touch others and give them hope when they are faced with what may seem like hopelessness. In all things, to God be the glory because great things He has done!

In March 2010, I was working in an administrative office for the University of Kentucky Hospital. Being a part of the hospital had its perks. One of which was the free flu shot we got each winter. This particular year, manufacturers came out with a flu shot that also promised a vaccine for the H1N1 flu, commonly known as "The Swine Flu." I remember standing in line with some of the ladies and joking around. "Wouldn't it be ironic if one of us got sick from getting a flu shot?"

I took the shot and went about my business. They told us that we might actually feel a little flu-like for a day or two. The vaccine actually gives you a small dose of the flu so that your system can build up immunity to it. Within three days, I remember feeling just really run down and tired. My right arm was kind of tingling and a little numb but I figured I'd just slept on it wrong. At night it was all I could do to crawl into bed and pass out.

On the third day after the flu shot, I went to work exhausted then back home to bed again. I awoke at about 8 PM with a sharp pain in my right arm. I knew something wasn't right. I stood to walk from the bedroom to the den where my wife, Elizabeth, was watching television with the kids. I was so tired that I had to walk down the hallway while leaning against the wall for support.

When I got into the better light of the den I looked down at my right arm and discovered that it was pasty-white and was curled up against my chest much like a stroke or palsy victim's arm would be positioned.

Elizabeth flew to my side and rushed me to the local emergency room. There they asked me the usual questions and ran some tests. After many hours they told me they weren't sure what I had. They said it was probably just a virus. They gave me an antibiotic and sent me home.

The next day I went back to work, but again, felt extremely fatigued. That evening I once again had a similar, yet worse reaction. The local doctors told Elizabeth that if it happened again to take me straight to the University of Kentucky's emergency room. She did and I was admitted, this time for five days.

When we arrived they ran all kinds of tests on me but could find nothing that really stood out. One doctor eventually told me, "We can now tell you of ten or fifteen thousand things that you don't have—but we're still not sure what is causing your pain and numbness. Usually we'd have already sent you home by now, but you are such a fascinating case that we want to run as many tests as we can!"

As a last effort they even scheduled me for a muscle biopsy surgery. They put me under anesthesia and took a section of muscle out of my thigh to test it. Eventually I was discharged and sent home, still unsure what caused my episode. The doctors reasoned I must have some strain of a virus, so they gave me a steroid regimen to take at home for seven to ten days and I faithfully took the steroid as prescribed.

I didn't realize it at the time, but that course of action was just about the most dangerous thing I could have done. A steroid, by nature, masks the symptoms of your illness. I assumed I was getting better but when the pills were gone the pain was back with a vengeance and this time it was different. Very different.

I remember getting out of bed and falling to the floor. Next I crawled to the hallway and finally tried to stand but couldn't do it. I couldn't even put one foot in front of the other. I fell again and tried to crawl to Elizabeth. I must have screamed for help. She came running and once again rushed me back to the emergency room. Elizabeth called my parents to let them know I was going back to the hospital and they drove up from Nashville to make sure I was all right. What unfolded next seems like something right out of a movie, but I truly know that God had a hand in it.

The University of Kentucky is a teaching hospital. One of the interns, that had studied my case when I was admitted the week before, saw that I had been brought in again. Something about my condition didn't sit right with her so she came down to check on me. After a quick examination she thought that I might have what's called "compartment syndrome" and did a pressure test on my legs and arms to verify. I was in so much agony that I don't remember much of that. They stuck a needle in my legs and arms to measure oxygen levels in my muscles. What she discovered alarmed her to such an extent that she ran to get another doctor.

In just a few short moments Elizabeth, my father, and I were facing yet another doctor but this time with a very grim prognosis.

"Mr. Shelby, you have compartment syndrome. It's in an acute stage. If we don't get you on an operating table within thirty minutes you are going to lose your legs. And if we're not successful with that you will probably lose your arms too."

I was stunned. "No, no. I just have a virus. That's what they've told me."

He went on to explain that the Swine Flu vaccine I took must have reacted with a virus that lay dormant in my system causing a super virus, a muscle-wasting virus. He quickly explained that my muscles were dying. They were no longer getting oxygen. And, that they needed to open up my legs and maybe my arms to allow oxygen to get directly to those muscles before gangrene set in. And that if too much gangrene had already occurred they'd have to amputate to keep it from spreading.

So for the second time in a little over a week I was once again on the operating table and I was scared to death.

Little did I know this was only the beginning of a harrowing journey.

Compartment Syndrome is a condition brought about by repetitive stress injuries. It is very rare but it can sometimes occur in construction workers or athletes. Soccer players might get it in their shins while football players sometimes get it in their shoulders. You get the idea.

This is one illness where the cure is just as bad or worse than the illness. Usually the unlucky victim gets it in only one place or muscle quadrant. In very rare cases someone might get it in two places. Lucky me, I got it in four—both legs, both arms.

Your muscles have a film around them that lets in oxygen but keeps out harmful impurities. Compartment Syndrome causes the film surrounding those muscle quadrants to harden, thus depriving your muscles of much needed oxygen. When the muscles cease to get oxygen they very quickly begin to die and decompose. This is when infectious gangrene sets in. If not caught very quickly, the infection usually is nearly fatal within three days. By my count I probably had Compartment Syndrome going on ten days by the time they did the surgery. Scared to death didn't even begin to describe what I was feeling.

The treatment for Compartment Syndrome is a surgical procedure called a fasciotomy. Any fisherman worth his salt knows this process because they basically gut you like a fish!

In my case, they cut two long **and** deep incisions on each leg from the side ankle up nearly to the bottom of the kneecap on the outside half of each leg, and the same incision on the inside half of each leg. They did the same with each of my arms. They cut a long and deep incision on the top of each arm from the wrist up to the elbow, then cut a long and deep incision on the bottom side of each arm from the wrist, again all the way up to the elbow. The goal is to expose as much muscle to oxygen as quickly as possible.

The recovery is excruciatingly painful. I had eight huge incisions all at the same time and they cannot stitch you up. They do not want to close the wounds for fear that the process might begin again. So you must lay in a hospital bed completely immobile with your wounds open and exposed, hoping to heal from the inside out.

One of the consequences of having to be sliced into so quickly is that they sliced right through many of the nerves in my arms and legs. I say many, but not all. I could still feel plenty, trust me. But when in recovery, I discovered that I could no longer move my fingers or feet and toes. The doctors explained that the nerves actually have to regrow and this could take extensive time. There was a probability that they may not even reconnect at all.

So there I lay in the hospital for weeks on end. As I said before, I tried to be a model patient. Elizabeth and I decided that we were going through it together and that we'd face whatever came. We got to know many of the nurses and techs really well. Many came to see me simply out of curiosity. My case was a total rarity. They even wrote medical papers about it.

Some of the medical students even came by just to have me show them my wounds. You could look right into them and see all the muscles, tendons, veins, nerves and bone—just like you were looking at a cadaver in a lab. They'd hold up my arm and watch the tendons move as I'd move what I could of my hands and wrist. They'd never seen such a thing on a "live" person before. Ha!

As I said, we got to know many of the hospital workers. Elizabeth and I decided that we wanted to use this illness to positively impact others, if possible. In short order, we went out of our way to get to know people. We found out where our doctors were from, what their hometowns were famous for, where they liked to shop... They all marveled at how well I was getting along. Whenever possible, we made sure to let them know that we had a Christian faith that sustained and uplifted us. We even had nurses that would come to my room in tears and ask us to pray for them because they were facing a hard night with patients that weren't so nice. God has a funny way of taking things like that and turning them around. Who'd have ever thought the patient would become the counselor?

So many from our church and work came by to see me. I had a steady stream of visitors so I always felt pressure to be "positive and upbeat." I wanted to be a comforter. I knew that people who saw me were shocked. Most tried to hide it but I'd see them wiping away a tear when they thought I wasn't looking. After a time it took a real effort to always be so positive and friendly. It seemed I was not getting better and I couldn't seem to move much of my legs and hands.

I tried as much as possible not to be a bother. I rarely called the nurses. One evening a nurse came in and opened the window by my bed so I could get some fresh air. She left and it started raining. I called the nurses station but no one came to close the window for over two hours. I just laid there getting soaked, unable to move and "fix" the simple problem for myself. Try as I might to stay positive, discouragement and depression seeped in.

I never blamed God for my illness but I found it increasingly difficult to keep up the act of being "Mr. Positive Christian." Still there are so many examples of how God took care of me and watched over me during that time.

In the early days after my initial surgery the doctors had to give me a lot of blood and plasma. They were constantly coming to change to a fresh supply. My mother was with me and noticed that my bed was continuously soaked in blood. She worried that I was losing too much blood. Ever positive, I assured her that I was fine and it was normal for the experience. She cried and cried, "This is not normal and I am going to get someone!"

That someone turned out to be my father. He took one look at me and yelled for the doctor, who came in and quickly determined that I was bleeding way too much, too fast. He called for a nurse, but none came. My father went to find a nurse but inexplicably none were available or around at the precise moment. The doctor determined that he had to get it stopped right at that moment with no time to wait any longer for a nurse. He asked my dad to assist him and handed him a pair of surgical gloves.

Right there in my room they both worked to stop the bleeding inside of my arms and legs. I was awake for the whole thing and I learned a lot about a father's love that day. Could you imagine being put in a similar situation? Dad held my wounds open with his own hands while the doctor worked with a small heat stick to stop the pressure points that were bleeding inside my wounds.

Most fathers, of course, would rush to do just the same and that really teaches me something about God too. God the Father had just the same emotions and feelings we would have when His own Son faced the cross. Everything in Him must have desired to rush to His side to save Him from that agony. Yet scripture says that it pleased God to allow Him to suffer because of His great love not only for Christ, but for what His sacrifice would mean for me and you. To me, this is one of the mysteries of God's nature. How could he be both Holy and Righteous while at the same time full "Abba, Father," or daddy? How did he do it?

So many things I could write about that hospital stay. So many miracles happened. Not the least of which was that in all that time I never got an infection. They watched me pretty closely and were fearful that an infection in my exposed state could be very bad, even deadly. Elizabeth was also such a help to me. God truly put us together. She has a faith that is amazing. And she shouldered all the burden of keeping up with the house, the kids, a job, church, and still managed to always be at my side when I needed her most.

I remember a time in the day after surgery. As you could imagine I was in great pain. Wait, you are surely thinking, "Mark, with the wounds you had, I bet they had you on so much medicine you couldn't feel a thing!" Wrong. Very wrong. They had me on a lot of medicine, but it was never enough. The pain was excruciating. It was unbearable. There were times when I truly thought I would lose my mind.

They had a pain management team dedicated to monitoring me around the clock. They even put one of those morphine pumps at my bed with instructions that I could press it every six minutes as needed for pain. Except there was one problem: I couldn't move my fingers to press the pump! They taped it to my hand and told me to just do the best I could. I laid there in agony. I'll tell you the truth; I wanted to die. Elizabeth had to push the button every six minutes for me. Finally, when I could take it no more I called the pain management team member to my bedside to beg and plead for something else for the pain. He leaned down very close to my face so no one else could hear and said in a low voice, *"Mr. Shelby, we're giving you everything we've got. Maximum dose of everything we can all at the same time. In your IV, you've got morphine, lortab, and several other painkillers. We're also feeding you "delotted."— it's the most potent pain medicine we have for you, but even on top of that we are actually giving you Ketamine, which is used around here as a horse tranquilizer. Mr. Shelby, there is nothing else to give you. If I had one tenth of what you have in your system I'd be dead on the floor. You're just going to have to make it on your own."*

He told Elizabeth not to worry about the "six-minute" rule, to push the morphine button as often as I needed it. I came to know pain on a pretty personal level.

But as much as there were dark days, God always placed good Christian people in my path to lift me up. My pastors and church friends were there to sit with me. I'm guessing they must have thought I was going through a "Job" experience! But God uses ordinary people to accomplish extraordinary things. If you think you are ordinary, keep a sharp eye! God may just allow you to be a miracle for someone else in their time of need!

Speaking of miracles, let me tell you about a hospital kitchen worker named Toby Mundy. Every day, he would call me up to get my meal order, "My man, Mr. Shelby! Named like one of the coolest cars, the Shelby Mustang GT. What can I get you for breakfast / lunch / dinner? The menu says such and such, but that's no good. You can have anything you want. Just name it. What can I bring you?" Then about thirty minutes later he'd come up with the tray and we'd talk. He saw my Bible and commented that he was a Christian too. We talked about favorite scriptures.

One morning, I was having a particularly tough time. I was in a lot of pain and was pretty depressed too. It was one of those dark hours I wrote about. One of the darkest. I didn't want Elizabeth to see me go through that so I sent her down to the hospital cafeteria to get her own breakfast. When she left, I lay in bed pleading with God to take me, if only he would. I said, "God, I'm not going to make it on my own. I can't do it. I need to know that you care about what's happening to me and I need to know it now. I need you now, Lord."

As I write this little story within my story, I am fighting back tears even now because I realize the incredible things that God can do when necessary. As I laid in my bed, from down the hall I heard Toby's voice singing as he was working, bringing meals to every patient on his hall.

"Why should I feel discouraged? Why do the shadows come?
Why does my heart feel lonely, and long for heaven and home?
When Jesus is my portion....A constant friend is He.
His eye is on the sparrow, and I know He watches me.
I sing because I'm happy! I sing because I'm free!
His eye is on the sparrow, and I know he watches me!"

God's timing is incredible! I knew that was a direct answer to my prayer! Toby came into my room and I said, "Toby, you'll never know what you meant to me today. I believe God placed you here this morning in answer to my prayers. I am having a really tough morning and I wouldn't usually ask, but would you mind if you and I sang just a verse of "Amazing Grace" together as a prayer offering and blessing for this breakfast?"

He smiled really big and we both sang "Amazing Grace" in two-part harmony with more emotion and feeling than either of us probably ever had. Well, probably three-part harmony because I know the Holy Spirit was in the room with us!

When we had finished Toby put his hand on my shoulder and said, "You're going to make it, Mark. God's telling me and I just know it."

He went on to minister to me by relating his own serious illness from just a few months before. He'd had pneumonia that turned into a collapsed lung situation, which then got infected. He very nearly died and spent time in the hospital too. During that time, he rededicated his life to serving The Lord by serving those he'd come into contact with at the hospital.

So whether you are a surgeon or CEO, a cook or a kitchen helper, God can use you mightily! I got the opportunity to talk to the chief administrator of the hospital; and told him about how much it meant to me to have someone of Toby's character working for the hospital. I assured him that he had done as much for me as any surgeon and I hoped he'd be recognized for it.

So many stories of people who "just happened" to be in the right place at exactly the right time—Always there when I needed them most.

After eight or nine weeks, I was finally fit enough to go home. There, I would have to stay for another four or five weeks before I could resume "life" as I'd come to know it. Through my hospital time and rehabilitation I had many challenges; not the least of which was learning to put weight on my legs and walk again.

I eventually regained the use of my hands and fingers, but the muscle and nerve damage in my legs was too severe. I can't move my toes very much and really have very little balance. They did nerve studies and discovered once again that I am a living, breathing, walking, and talking miracle. The doctor said I have sustained permanent muscle damage over about eight-percent of my body and that it is so extensive that I really shouldn't have made it through the ordeal at all. Once again, I got the opportunity to tell him just how good my God truly is!

Going back to work was difficult—nearly impossible. The first week back I sat at my desk in tortured pain all day. It simply hurt too much to sit upright or stand for any period of time. I had a few good friends that were very supportive but some days it was all I could do to sit at my desk and fight back the tears. Often I'd go into a quiet office to just lie down for fifteen or twenty minutes. It was just simply too much. I was not successful at enduring the physical pain, and once more, the doubt, depression and fear crept in.

One such morning, I was driving to work and it was all I could do to keep my hands on the steering wheel. I had told Elizabeth I was fine to drive myself because I wanted it to be true. But I was not fine. I was driving down a highway, spiraling into excruciating pain very quickly. I was in trouble and could barely press the gas or the brake pedals. I instinctively knew that by my own strength I wouldn't make it... and if I didn't make it to the job, I was going to turn around, go back home, give up on life and lay on the couch. Don't ask me how I knew that, I just did. I did the only thing I knew to do. I cried out to God, "Lord, I need you right now!"

At that very moment, a brilliant white dove swooped down in front of my vehicle. It hovered there in front of my windshield as I was driving about fifty miles per hour down the road. I don't know how I knew it was a dove, but I instinctively knew that it was. It was the most brilliant shade of white I had ever seen. It almost glowed as it swooped and flitted between my vehicle and a mid-size truck in the right lane next to me. Back and forth, it went between him and me as we drove down the highway. The other driver looked at me with big eyes; and I looked at him. We both just grinned. He knew as well as I did that this was something way out of the "ordinary."

We drove on like this for several miles with the dove continually in front of me. The whole time I simply kept my eye on the dove. After a bit I started to worry about the bird. "How in the world was it flying so fast for so long? I was afraid that I was going to give it a heart attack so I slowly pulled off to the shoulder of the road. The dove flew off with me; then it flew down into a field where it seemed to vanish in a small grove of trees. I looked up to see I was right at the off ramp exit for my work! I sat in my car stunned and shaking. The only words I could say were, "Lord, did I just see an angel? Did I just see Your Holy Spirit? I know I did! You met me just when I needed you most! Praise God! Praise God! Praise God! You are holy! You are great!" It was just all I could figure out to say.

I have had the opportunity to share my story several times and I always do. I make sure that the person I'm telling it to knows that if it weren't for God's grace, I wouldn't be who I am, what I am, or where I am today. Without fail, people have always thanked me for sharing my story.

Not long after I returned to work, my Uncle Mike's southern gospel singing group, Eternal Vision, was performing near my home so I went to see them. I told him a few of the miracles that I had experienced and how God had seen me through some really tough days. He asked if he could share my testimony that night with the audience. When the service was over, he told me that a woman had approached him afterward and confided that she was going through a lot in her life too. In fact, she had even considered suicide and had made up her mind to attempt it. After she heard my testimony about God's goodness and faithfulness, she said she put away such thoughts and decided then and there to continue on and wait for God to work in her life.

My story is a hard one with lessons learned. Plenty of people have suffered worse than I did, I'm sure. But God has been faithful and I have tried to remain faithful to the promise I made to my Papaw on one of those darkest days. I have tried to make sure that God gets the glory and honor and praise anytime I retell it.

As for my own progress, I've come to terms with the fact that I'll never be what I once was. And thank God for it! They fitted me with braces for my legs and I sometimes walk with a cane when I get fatigued. The pain is sometimes still rough. It usually comes now in spasms. But in a way, I find it an honor to suffer and consider it as Paul did, a "thorn in my flesh" given to me as a reminder of God's faithfulness.

Today, I take great joy in serving others. I know what they are going through and I love to pray with them and for them. I'm so thankful that God gave me this testimony to tell and to use for His glory! And I have discovered that when you release that kind of selfishness and pride that God can truly transform your life. He did mine and I still have so much to let go of and so much still yet to do!

In fact, I am sure that He has a work for me to do. I feel called to tell my story and preach His word when given the opportunity. God has truly done a work in my life. My own home church sensed such a profound change in me that they ordained me a deacon. I am most pleased with the opportunities that have opened up for me to continue to serve and support others.

One of my first Sunday's back to church after my recovery, I was given the opportunity to give a quick testimony and sing a song for the congregation. The song, "More than ever" by the Gaithers mirrored so much of what I had experienced.

Thank you, Papaw for giving me the chance to put down on paper what has meant so much to me. I hope you will be able to use some of my testimony and I am really proud to be known as one of your "sons!"

Mark Shelby, February 2014

Part III: Letters

Children Thankful for Service

These letters have been written with great love by the students at Robert E. Aylor Middle School. I was blessed to accompany 128 students as we welcomed Edie and her 5th group of veterans to the World War II Memorial in October of 2014. When they heard I was planning on surprising Edie when she came up in April, they begged to write letters since they could not come with me this time. Although we have never met you, each and every one of you hold a special place in our hearts. We would all like to thank you from the bottom of our hearts for your service to our great country.

Dear Mr Shelby,

My name is Thomas. I am very grateful that you did what you did in World War Two. I am in 6th grade, I am 11 years old, and I am honored that you were there to help protect the world. I thank you for protecting my future and the worlds future. Thank you for being there for the world and I really appreciate what you did to win and I hope that you will write back.

Dear Wiley Shelby,

Thank you for serving our country you have done so much for our country. Thank you for make world peace. You have made this world a better place. What did it feel like when you have came home? Do you feel good knowing that you have done something good for the world. I think you have. Thank you for serving our county you have made a difference in the world.

Sincerely,

Serenity

Dear Mr. Shelby,

Thank you for your service. I am very grateful that you served in the war for our country. You have helped to shape our nation and to protect it. I am proud that there are people in our country brave enough to fight for us. I want you to know that I appreciate you and all the other people who have fought for our country. The United States would not be the same without you. Thank you.

Sincerely,

Isabella

Letter From a Neighbor

This letter is from our neighbors after my Imogene passed away.

The Lord said, "Love thy neighbor as thyself." These neighbors live two doors down the street from us. If all neighbors were like that the lock and security companies would be out of business. I would like to share the letter with you to the glory of God.

This is what God can do with you if you fully surrender yourself to Him. Present your body a living sacrifice. Be not conformed to this world, but be ye transformed by the renewing of your mind.

April 30, 2014

Minister Wiley Shelby,

Just a line to say hello and we are thinking about you and the family, but most of all we are praying for the family. We can't put enough words together to show our deepest sympathy but Jesus. Pastor Shelby, everything I'm saying you know more about than I can say about the one that hung on that old rugged cross. He's a heart fixer and a mind regulator. We pray that all of the years of together can be some enjoyable memory. Prayer is our source of communication with our Heavenly Father. In the midst of tribulations, faults and failures, Christ Jesus is only a prayer away, and He does all things well. As the song writer wrote, "What a friend we have in Jesus, all our sins and griefs to bear. What a privilege to carry everything to God in prayer." So hold on to God's unchanging hand, trusting in Him, who will never leave nor forsake you, whatever years may bring. May it be of inner strength, knowing your brother and sister in Christ are praying for the family. Pastor Shelby, if we can ever be of help to you in any way, we are just a phone call away.

Emma & George Tate

Part IV: Personal Thoughts and Sermon Notes

Wiley Shelby Contemplating

Don't Look Back

Don't lose your blessings and don't lose your faith, by looking at things that matter less than going forward toward home. Keep your focus on the goal set before you.

Now faith is the substance of things hoped for, the evidence of things not seen. (Hebrews 11:1)

Consider the story about a school holding a 100-yard dash. Some of the children started out but got distracted. They slowed down to look back and they got off track. They didn't reach the goal or receive a prize because they failed to focus on the end goal.

Many Christians get distracted in the same way. This happens in our spiritual life when we look back constantly and become preoccupied with our past and the stumbling blocks Satan puts in our path. We don't reach our objective. Paul reminds us in Philippians 3 to leave the past behind—look forward to what lies ahead in order to obtain the prize of the heavenly call of God in Christ Jesus. In verses 13-14, Paul says "...but this one thing I do, forgetting those things which are behind and reaching forth unto those things which are before. I press toward the mark for the prize of the high calling. Satan tempts us to turn back but there is nothing to go back to. (Luke 9:62) Jesus said, "No man having put his hand to the plough, and looking back is fit for the Kingdom of God.

The Children of Israel became discouraged. They wanted to go back to Egypt for cucumbers and melons. They forgot the bondage and where they were headed, the land where milk & honey flow. Where they could own their land. Where they could be free to worship God. But through their disobedience they spent 40 years wandering in the wilderness. Even then, God cared for them. While there, their clothes and shoes didn't wear out! God fed them quail and manna from heaven. But due to disobedience, only two adults that left Egypt, Joshua and Caleb, entered the Promised Land, along with their children.

Don't look back! Move forward to the goal set before you. I sure wouldn't want to miss the promises of God because of disobedience!

Just think, Jesus promised us a home with Him in Heaven for eternity—where there is no sickness, no sorrow, no pain, no little graves on the hillside, no hunger. All will be joy there with the Lord. Oh how I love to read John's gospel chapter 14 and Revelation of the promises God has made to His Born-again Believers.

Don't Quit

During the years of Imogene's dialysis, I wondered how things would be if she wouldn't listen to me every time she said "I am just going to quit going to dialysis." And I would respond, "Don't give up. Don't quit. We have come too far to quit now! We said 'til death do us part over 70 years ago. So hang on, the road is rough but we will make it through." Sometimes I felt that way but it would have been worse without her. Don't quit!

Life gets tedious with its twists and turns—something just about everyone learns—many failures come about just because they didn't stick it out. Don't give up though the digging is slow. Just one more foot and the well may blow. Success is failure turned wrong side out. The silver lining of the clouds of doubt, so don't quit. You might be closer when it seems far out. So don't quit. When it is a hard road, be ready to shout for that is what it is all about. Don't quit!

Hard times

Feb 6, 2014, it's a cold morning as I try to get Imogene to eat her breakfast. Something she said reminded me of a song I heard when I was a little boy in Union County.

It's hard times in Maynardville Jail. It's hard times, poor boy.
The stuff we eat is not too sweet.
It's old cornbread and old fat meat.
They bring it to the cell in an old tin pan.
You eat it the best way you can.
It's hard times in Maynardville Jail. It's hard times, poor boy.
...

Back then, songs told a story. Maybe it helped to sing that kind of songs to my kids while they were growing up. As far as I know, not one of my kids spent a night in jail. Thank God! So you see it is true: Train up a child in the way he should go and when he is old he will not depart from it.

More evidence of the truth of this scripture: My son Mike called to say they just got back home from a cruise to the Bahamas where they sang and witnessed to people there and on the ship. The Eternal Vision quartet is Mike, his wife Gail, his son Shannon, and Stuart Stallings. But the main conductor of the group is the Lord God.

Sin Just Doesn't Pay

(II Samuel 11 & 12)

When David saw Bathsheba on the roof taking a bath, he should have been in the battle! He was in the wrong place at the wrong time! He should have been where God wanted him to be. The blackest spot in David's life, adultery, virtual murder to cover up adultery, and his remorse made him a broken man. God forgave him, but pronounced judgment on him. "The sword shall never leave thy house," and it never did.

David reaped what he had sown. What a long hard harvest: His daughter Tamar was raped by her brother Amon, who in turn was murdered by their brother Absalom. Absalom led a rebellion against his father, David, and was killed in the struggle to take the king's place. David's wives were violated in public, as he had secretly violated the wife of Uriah. David's reign was clouded with trouble. Some people think they can sin, sin, sin and get by with it. Even though David was the man after God's own heart, he didn't get by without paying dearly with tears & pain.

You must be born again

(John 3)

All have sinned and come short of the glory of God but redemption is available to all who come to Christ seeking forgiveness.

Jesus told Nicodemus, "Ye must be born again."

Many people think that as long as they do good works, pay tithes, and give to the poor they can live like they want to live and somehow make it into heaven. But not so: you must be born again. You must realize that you are lost and repent. Like the woman at the well—Jesus told her of her sin. She had five husbands and the one she was living with was not her husband. He told her everything she had done. He knows everything about you and me. Nothing is hidden.

In Luke 15, the prodigal son thought he could do whatever he wanted and get by. He wasted his entire inheritance and a big part of his life before he came to his senses. He saw himself in the pig pen and repented before his Father. Like him, please talk to God before you lose your mind or your life. Today is the day of salvation. Come now, let us reason together says the Lord.

For the wages of sin is death; but the gift of God is eternal life through Jesus Christ our Lord. (Romans 6:23)

Consider your inheritance

Sometimes we lose sight of Heaven by becoming totally consumed by things of this world: fine cars, luxury homes, money, jewels, social rank, and careers. None of these are really bad or evil but they can become our idols or little gods if we focus on them. God made us to share His kingdom. Everything belongs to Him including our love and devotion. God is number one.

Nothing can separate us from the love of God. We cannot be plucked from His hand. We have a heavenly home that Paul says, "Eyes have not seen, neither ears heard, nor had it entered in the heart of man what is in store for those who love the LORD." (1 Corinthians 2:9)

1 Peter 1 describes our incorruptible inheritance. When we are born again by grace through faith in Jesus Christ, we become heirs to the kingdom of God and that means joint heirs with Jesus. He became the means of our salvation through His death and resurrection. We have a living hope in Him, not a dead one, for He lives. John 14 tells us our new home is a better place: "In my Father's house are many mansions" and "I go to prepare a place for you." He will come back for me and all believers, to live with us for eternity! It is reserved for me! It is undefiled, will not fade away, incorruptible and eternal! And I am kept by the power of God through faith unto salvation; ready to be with Him when He comes.

Think on Jesus and what He did for you and me!

The Charge for Deacons

Acts chapter 6 tells us two reasons why the early church set aside Deacons:

1. Promoting the growth of the Kingdom

2. Murmuring of some that the church was being inconsistent in its care of widows

Deacons are to be men full of the Holy Ghost and wisdom.

Models of the Early Church Deacons:

Read Acts 7:51-60

Stephen was the first Church martyr. He preached the gospel and was arrested and stoned for his commitment.

Read Acts 8

Philip was totally committed to God. He preached the great revival at Samaria during the era of Christian persecution, and left to minister to one Ethiopian in the desert, as directed by God.

The office of Deacon is not only a place of honor, but a place of service. Originally the Deacons assumed the responsibilities of visitation and general care of the church. This is the only purpose of their existence. For those who move to this high place of service the following requirements are necessary.

1. He should live a consecrated Christian life, bringing no reproach by his conduct upon the church or the cause of Christ.

2. He should attend church every Sunday morning and Sunday night, Wednesday night and fully participate in all special church meetings, unless hindered by some reason which is approved by his good conscience.

3. He should bring his tithe systematically to the church to do the Lord's work.

4. He should be evangelistic and missionary in spirit, deeply interested in the salvation of souls at home and abroad.

5. He should be fully cooperative with the pastor and church in a great spiritual program of advancement.

6. He should refrain from destructive criticism of his pastor and church or its leadership, willing to settle all difficulties in a quiet and Christian manner, without hurting the cause of Christ and His church, building up the Church.

7. He should keep in trust and confidentiality those things which should only be discussed in private.

8. He should be active in the various educational programs of the church, including Sunday School and church training.

9. He should be perceived as "a good Christian man" in the community, church, workplace, etc.

10. He should measure up to the requirements given in I Timothy 3:8-13, "being found blameless."

11. He should remember James 1:27. "Pure religion and undefiled before God and the Father is this, to visit the fatherless and widows in their affliction, and to keep himself unspotted from the world."

Summary: A Deacon called of God should be a man of dignity.

Sample Ordination Service

This is an example of an ordination service.

Accepting the Call to the Gospel Ministry

What should we do when faced with important responsibilities?

- We must first turn from self-reliance to depend on God.

- We must focus on what is important to God.

- We must demonstrate love and faith, by walking with God, rather than to please ourselves.

God gives us opportunities to serve Him in bearing important responsibilities to our home, to our church, at our work, in our community, and in our nation. As we turn to Him, He gives us wisdom and helps us. As believers,

- We must never give in to Satan.

- We must always affirm the virgin birth of Jesus Christ, His substitutionary death on the cross, His resurrection and the Truth. He is coming again for His people; and

- We must refuse to compromise **the Truth of the Gospel**.

John 3:16 For God so loved the world that he gave his only begotten Son, that whosoever believeth in Him should not perish, but have everlasting life. **17** For God sent not his Son into the world to condemn the world; but that the world through Him might be saved.

Acts4:10 Be it known unto you all, and to all the people of Israel, that by the name of Jesus Christ of Nazareth, whom ye crucified, whom God raised from the dead, even by him doth this man stand here before you whole. **11** This is the stone which was set at naught of you builders, which is become the Head of the corner. **12** Neither is there salvation in any other: for there is none other name under heaven given among men, whereby we must be saved.

1 Timothy 2:5 For there is one God, and one mediator between God and men, the man Christ Jesus.

"It is a privilege to give you this Charge."

The Charge

2 Timothy 4:1 I charge thee therefore before God, and the Lord Jesus Christ, who shall judge the quick and the dead at His appearing and his kingdom; **2** Preach the word; be instant in season, out of season; reprove, rebuke, exhort with all longsuffering and doctrine. **3** For the time will come when they will not endure sound doctrine; but after their own lusts shall they heap to themselves teachers, having itching ears; **4** And they shall turn away their ears from the truth, and shall be turned unto fables. **5** But watch thou in all things, endure afflictions, do the work of an evangelist, make full proof of thy ministry.

1 Timothy 3:2 A bishop must be blameless, the husband of one wife, vigilant, sober, of good behavior, given to hospitality, apt to teach;

Acts 20:28 Take heed therefore unto yourselves, and to all the flock, over which the Holy Ghost hath made you overseers, to feed the church of God, which he hath purchased with his own blood.

1 Peter 5:2 Feed the flock of God which is among you, taking the oversight thereof, not by constraint, but willingly; not for filthy lucre, but of a ready mind; **3** Neither as being lords over God's heritage, but being examples to the flock. **4** And when the chief Shepherd shall appear, ye shall receive a crown of glory that fadeth not away. **5** Likewise, ye younger, submit yourselves unto the elder. Yea, all of you be subject one to another, and be clothed with humility: for God resisteth the proud, and giveth grace to the humble. **6** Humble yourselves therefore under the mighty hand of God, that He may exalt you in due time: **7** Casting all your care upon Him; for He careth for you. **8** Be sober, be vigilant; because your adversary the devil, as a roaring lion, walketh about, seeking whom he may devour: **9** Whom resist steadfast in the faith, knowing that the same afflictions are accomplished in your brethren that are in the world. **10** But the God of all grace, who hath called us unto His eternal glory by Christ Jesus, after that ye have suffered a while, make you perfect, establish, strengthen, and settle you.

Matthew 29:19 Go ye therefore, and teach all nations, baptizing them in the name of the Father, and of the Son, and of the Holy Ghost. **20** Teaching them to observe all things whatsoever I have commanded you: and lo, I am with you always, even unto the end of the world. Amen.

"Go With God's Blessings."

A Man Who Took Something with Him When He Died

The Rich Man in Hell

Read Luke 16

1. Let's take notice what the rich man left behind when he went to hell.

> a) He left behind all his money. He left behind every penny he had and so will you.

> b) He left his five brothers behind.

> c) He left all his fine clothes behind. He had been clothed in purple and fine linen.

> d) He left his life of ease and comfort and sumptuous living. In verse 25 it says, "Thou in your lifetime received the good things, but now you are tormented. Likewise Lazarus received evil things, and now he is comforted."

2. Let's take notice what he took with him when he went to Hell.

> a) His senses. He took at least four senses to hell.

>> 1. His power to feel. He was tormented in flames.

>> 2. His power to see. He saw Father Abraham afar off with Lazarus in his bosom.

>> 3. His power to speak. He cried to Father Abraham to have mercy on him, that he

might send Lazarus to dip the tip of his finger in water to cool his tongue, for he was tormented in the flames.

4. His power to hear. He heard the voice of Abraham say, "Son, remember you had good things and Lazarus evil."

b) He took his memory. He possibly was remembering how he treated Lazarus at his gate. He wouldn't do anything for Lazarus while they both were living. And now he wanted Lazarus to help, but he couldn't. The dogs treated Lazarus better by licking his sores.

c) He took his ability to pray. The first thing he did in hell was pray—but too late.

d) He took his concern for his five brothers who were on their way to hell.

e) He took his unchanged nature to hell with him forever.

3. Let's take notice what he found when he went to hell.

a) First thing was that hell was a real place! In hell he lifted up his eyes in torment.

b) He found a place of suffering. He said, "I am tormented in this flame."

c) He found a place of no mercy, no love, no forgiveness. He cried, "Father Abraham, have mercy on me." But the door of God's mercy was forever closed to him.

But the door of God's mercy is still open to you if and when you surrender your life to Jesus Christ.

It doesn't matter if you are rich or poor. If you neglect His gift of salvation, say no to accepting Jesus Christ as your Savior, reject Him and hell is your destiny.

Today is the day of salvation. "Be ye also ready, as you know not the day or hour when Jesus will come." If you have taken Him as your personal savior you **will** go to Heaven. If not, think about the horror of hell, the pain and agony there. Then think about Heaven and being with Jesus and having joy, peace and happiness.

John 3:3 Jesus said, "Verily, verily, I say unto thee, except a man be born again, he cannot see the Kingdom of God." That seems very plain to me. How about you?

The Best Trade You Ever Made

John 1:35-42

The two disciples and John saw Jesus as He was walking. John said, "Behold the Lamb of God." The two disciples heard him speak and they followed Jesus. Jesus turned and saw them following and sayeth unto them, "What seek ye?" They said unto Him, "Rabbi," which means Master, "Where dwellest thou?" He said unto them, "Come and see." They saw where He dwelt and abode with Him that day, for it was about the tenth hour. One of the two which heard John speak and followed Him was Andrew, Simon Peter's brother. He first findeth his own brother, Simon, and sayeth unto him, "We have found the Messiah," which is Christ. And he brought him to Jesus, and when Jesus beheld him, he said, "Thou art Simon, the son of Jonas. Thou shalt be called Cephas", which means a stone.

Everybody seems to be interested in a good deal. But it seems that most people are interested in material things. Not many Christians seem to be interested in improving their spiritual lives.

1. The best deal is salvation.

> How shall we escape if we neglect so great a salvation? (Hebrews 2:3)

a) Trade Satan for Salvation

b) Trade Sin for Salvation

c) Trade Sadness for a Song; joy, comfort, blessing and the promises of God.

2. The bargain in your daily service

I am come that they might have life and that they might have it more abundantly. (John 10:10)

a) It's a bargain if you live for Jesus like you lived for Satan

b) It's a bargain if you love the lost like you used to love sin.

c) It's a bargain if you lift up the Savior like you used to lift up the devil.

3. The Bible instead of the battle with the Spirit

The Law of the Lord is perfect, converting the soul; the testimony of the Lord is sure, making wise the simple. The statutes of the Lord are right, rejoicing the heart; the commandment of the Lord is pure, enlightening the eyes; the fear of the Lord is clean, enduring forever; the judgments of the Lord are true and righteous altogether. More to be desired are they then gold, yea, then much fine gold, sweeter also than honey and the honeycomb. Moreover by them is the servant warned and in keeping of them there is a great reward. (Psalm 19:7-11)

a) Exchange booze for the Bible

b) Exchange the world's failed promises for God's binding promises

c) Exchange position in the world for position in God's kingdom

    1. Moses exchanged the king's palace for God's promises

    2. Paul exchanged life as a Pharisee for a life in Christ

4. The blessings of the Lord instead of the burdens of Satan

> Paul said, "I am sure that when I come unto you, I shall come in the fullness of the blessings of the gospel of Christ." (Romans 15:29)

> **a)** It's a good deal to change your lost state for a loving Savior.

> **b)** It's a good deal to change your life of slavery to Satan for a life of service to Christ.

> **c)** It's a good deal to change your life of leprosy of sin for the liberty of the Spirit.

> **d)** If the Son therefore will make you free, you shall be free indeed. (John 8:36)

> **e)** Paul said, "for the law of the Spirit of life in Christ Jesus hath made me free from the law of sin and death." (Romans 8:2)

> **f)** Paul said, "There is therefore now no condemnation to them which are in Christ Jesus, who walk not after the flesh, but after the Spirit." (Romans 8:1)

5. It's a good trade to exchange the ugliness of sin for the beauty of holiness.

> For the wages of sin is death, but the gift of God is eternal life through Jesus Christ our Lord. (Romans 6:23)

a) A good trade, your sickness for soundness.

b) A good trade, your shame for a smile.

c) A good trade, your sorrows for singing.

d) A good trade, hell for Heaven.

Jesus said, "For what does a man profit if he should gain the whole world, and lose his own soul? Or what should a man give in exchange for his own soul? (Matthew 16:26)

6. A good deal: Trade a burning hell for a home with the saints.

Let not your heart be troubled. Ye believe in God, believe also in me. In my Father's house are many mansions. If it were not so, I would have told you. I go to prepare a place for you. And if I go and prepare a place for you, I will come again, and receive you unto myself, that where I am, ye may be also. (John 14:1-2)

a) A good deal: trading decaying materials for a mansion in glory.

b) A good deal: trading death's madness for a life's measureless grace.

c) A good deal: trading a debt of misery for the Master's goodness.

We Need to Walk Like Jesus

The Spirit Himself testifies with our Spirit that we are God's children. (Romans 8:16)

Your enemy wants to steal your identify. Your identity will determine who you become. When God created man, He made him in the likeness of Himself. When Adam lived 130 years, he had a son in his own image. He named him Seth. (Genesis 5:1-3)

The enemy wants to create an identity crisis. Wake up, old sleeper, arise from the dead, and Christ will shine on you. Ephesians 5:14.

1. He wants to destroy our unity.

2. He wants to get you to sin a little.

3. He wants to lead you to false teachers.

Jesus opened his mouth and taught them. Matthew 5:13-16

He didn't teach man's way. He said, "You are the salt of the earth, but if the salt has lost its savor, it is good for nothing." A person who is out of fellowship with God is good for nothing spiritually. You can't serve God and mammon; either serve one or the other.

You are a light to the world. A lamp with no oil puts out no light. A man without the Lord is in darkness.

The sinner is watching your life, to see how you act. So stay in touch with God and let your light shine, that man may see your good works and glorify you father, who is in Heaven.

You can't bounce back and forth like a rubber ball and please God. A little sin is as bad as a big sin. It's all the same in the eyes of God. A Christian without the Holy Spirit has no light, no witness, no power.

Ye hypocrites, well did Esaias prophesy of you, saying, This people draweth nigh unto me with their mouth, and honoureth me with their lips; but their heart is far from me. But in vain they do worship me, teaching for doctrines the commandments of men. (Matthew 15:7-9)

Not every one that saith unto me, Lord, Lord, shall enter into the kingdom of heaven; but he that doeth the will of my Father which is in heaven. (Matthew 7:21)

Ye shall know them by their fruits. Do men gather grapes of thorns, or figs of thistles? Even so every good tree bringeth forth good fruit; but a corrupt tree bringeth forth evil fruit. A good tree cannot bring forth evil fruit, neither can a corrupt tree bring forth good fruit. (Matthew 7:16-18)

Many will say to me in that day, Lord, Lord, have we not prophesied in thy name? and in thy name have cast out devils? and in thy name done many wonderful works? And then will I profess unto them, I never knew you: depart from me, ye that work iniquity. (Matthew 7:22-23)

There is only one way to Heaven; that is **Jesus** Christ.

Enter in at the straight gate, for wide is the gate and broad is the way that leadeth to destruction. Many go in thereat. Because straight is the gate and narrow is the way which leadeth unto life and few find it. (Matthew 7:13-14)

Come to Christ now. **Today** is **the** day of salvation. Stake your claim in the blood of Jesus.

A Greater Kind of Love

The word "love" has different meanings for different people at different stages of life.

1. Before 5 years old a child wants the love of Mom and Dad.

2. About 5 years old a child wants the love of a puppy or kitten

3. About 10 years old you want the love of a friend.

4. At 15 years old you want the love of a boyfriend or a girlfriend—or a car.

5. At 20 you want to be married—like all your girlfriends.

6. At 30 you want the love of a family.

At different ages some people realize God's love is more important than the love of worldly things.

When we come to know the Lord as our Personal Savior, some young, some older, and we read the love chapter, we come to know what love really is: unconditional love from our Savior.

1 Corinthians 13

Though I speak with the tongues of men and of angels, and have not charity, I am become as sounding brass, or a tinkling cymbal. And though I have the gift of prophecy, and understand all mysteries, and all knowledge; and though I have all faith, so that I could remove mountains, and have not charity, I am nothing. And though I bestow all my goods to feed the poor, and though I give my body to be burned, and have not charity, it profiteth me nothing.

Charity suffereth long, and is kind; charity envieth not; charity vaunteth not itself, is not puffed up, doth not behave itself unseemly, seeketh not her own, is not easily provoked, thinketh no evil; rejoiceth not in iniquity, but rejoiceth in the truth; beareth all things, believeth all things, hopeth all things, endureth all things. Charity never faileth: but whether there be prophecies, they shall fail; whether there be tongues, they shall cease; whether there be knowledge, it shall vanish away. For we know in part, and we prophesy in part. But when that which is perfect is come, then that which is in part shall be done away.

When I was a child, I spake as a child, I understood as a child, I thought as a child: but when I became a man, I put away childish things. For now we see through a glass, darkly; but then face to face: now I know in part; but then shall I know even as also I am known.

And now abideth faith, hope, charity, these three; but the greatest of these is charity.

The Nature of God's Love

Text: 1 John 4:7-11

1. God's love is a saving love. When Jesus shed His blood on Calvary, He paid for the sins of the whole world. When we accept Him as our Savior, God accepts that payment, washes our sins away, saves us, transforms us, and takes us into His family.

For as many as received Him, to them gave He power to become the sons of God, even to them that believe on His name. (John 1:12)

Then tell me, is there any greater love than that?

2. God's love is a keeping love.

God loves the sinner, but Oh!! He has a peculiar love for the one who comes to Christ. He loves him so much, he will never allow him to go down to everlasting suffering.

3. God's love is a providing love.

But my God shall supply all your needs according to His riches in glory, by Jesus Christ. (Philippians 4:19)

What do you **need** today? Go to God for it. In love He will provide it. He will not give you all you want, for what you want may not be best for you. But He will give you all you need. He is our Creator and Savior. Come to Him in prayer. He loves you.

4. God's love is a comforting love.

No one can comfort you like God can. No one has known the sorrow that he knew. Jesus knows what it is to weep, for He wept over Jerusalem and Lazarus. He knows what it is for a friend to forsake Him. For His friend, Peter, denied Him and another, Judas Iscariot, betrayed Him.

5. God's love is a demanding love.

Down by the seaside, Jesus said to Peter three times, "Do you love me?" Peter vowed that he did. Then Jesus said to him, "Feed my sheep." He was simply saying to Peter what He is saying to us today. "If you love me, do something about it. "

6. God's love is an eternal love.

For God so loved the world, that He gave His only begotten Son, that whosoever believeth in him should not perish, but have everlasting life. (John 3:16)

Paul said, "And now abidith faith, hope, and love. But the greatest of these is love." (1 Corinthians 13:13)

You Can't Outrun or Hide From God

From the book of Jonah ...

There was a preacher man named Jonah. God told him to go to a city named Ninevah. This city had more than six-score thousand persons that could not discern between their right hand from their left. But God loved them and wanted Jonah to go and preach against their sinfulness. They were a wicked city.

But Jonah did not want to preach that message to them. So he went down and bought a ticket for Tarshish. He tried to hide from the presence of the Lord, but God knew where he was, down in the bottom of the ship, fast asleep.

So God sent out a big wind and storm upon the sea. The sailors were very afraid of the storm. Each prayed to their gods, but the storm continued. It was so bad that they feared for their lives. The ship master went down and woke Jonah. He told him to call on his Lord so that they might not perish.

They cast lots to see whose fault it was. The lot fell on Jonah. They asked him who he was, his name, and where he was from. He said, "I am a Hebrew and I fear the Lord God of Heaven, the one who made the land and sea." He told them that he fled from the presence of the Lord.

They wondered what they were going to do to cause the sea to calm down. "What have you done to cause this?" they asked of Jonah. He said he had fled from God. Then they asked him what they could do to calm the sea. Jonah told them that if they threw him overboard the sea will be calm because it was his fault. Nevertheless the men rowed faster to get the ship to land, but they could not. They cried to the Lord that He wouldn't let them perish for this man's life. Jonah told them to throw him overboard. When they did, the storm stopped.

Now the Lord had prepared a big fish to swallow up Jonah. Jonah was in the fish's belly three days and three nights. He said, "The water compassed him, the weeds wrapped about his head. The fish went down to the bottom of the mountains in the water, the earth, her bars were about him." Jonah's soul fainted within him. He said, "I remembered the Lord and I prayed and the Lord heard." The fish couldn't stand a backslidden preacher so God made the fish sick and he vomited him up out on dry land.

Jonah said unto the Lord, "I will sacrifice unto thee with my voice of Thanksgiving. I will pay what I have vowed. Salvation is of the Lord. I cried by reason of mine affliction unto the Lord, out of the belly of hell, and He heard my voice."

And the word of the Lord came to Jonah the second time, saying, "Arise, go to Ninevah. Preach to them what I bid you to tell them." So Jonah went like God said. Jonah went to Ninevah, great city of a three days' journey. He cried and said, "Yet forty days, Ninevah shall be overthrown." The people believed God, proclaimed a fast, and put on sackcloth, from the greatest to the least of them, even the king. The king rose from his throne. He laid down his robe, and sat in ashes. The king made a decree that neither man nor beast eat or drink, but have all be covered with sackcloth and ashes.

They turned from their evil ways and prayed to God. They repented of their evil ways. God saw their works and that they turned from evil to Him. God repented of the evil he had said he would do unto them and he did not.

This displeased Jonah. He was very angry and told the Lord that he knew this was going to happen. They were wicked and he didn't want them saved. He told God He knew he was a merciful God, gracious and slow to anger. Then he asked God to take his life.

God told him that he doest well to be angry. Jonah went out of the city and made a booth to sit under.

He wanted to know what would become of the city. God made a gourd to come up to shade Jonah. He was pleased for that, but God prepared a worm the next morning. It smote the gourd and it withered. When the sun rose God sent an east wind and it beat upon his head. He fainted. He wished to die. Then said the Lord, "You had pity on the gourd; you labored not nor made it grow. Should I not spare Ninevah with six-score thousand persons that cannot discern between their right hand and their left hand?"

What God Is Like

Jesus taught in parables.

He is my source for everything good. God is our Heavenly Father.

He is not a substitute, nor a mirage, nor a false god.

There is none like Him. He is a living God. He is alive. He is the Alpha and Omega, the Beginning and the End, the First and the Last.

1. God is like a Coke. He is the real thing.

2. God is like Pan Am. He makes the going great. No distance is too far for Him or too tough for Him to go. He went all the way to the Old Rugged Cross with His Son, to pay our sin debt. John 3:16.

3. God is like General Electric. He will light your path and lead you in it, and walk with you, if you will let Him.

4. God is like Bayer Aspirin. He works wonders. He can ease all pain. Just take a good dose of Him.

5. God is like Hallmark Cards. He cares enough to send the very best. He sent His only Son to pay our sin debt. Nothing or no one else could do the job.

6. God is like Tide washing powder. He gets out the stains that the other gods of this world leave behind.

7. God is like VO5 hair spray. He holds through all kinds of storms in our lives if you believe and ask Him to.

8. God is like Dial soap. Aren't you glad you know Him? Don't you wish everybody did? What a better place this world would be if everyone were true Christians.

9. God is like Sears Roebuck. He has everything and anything you need. Just ask Him.

10. God is like Alka-seltzer. Try Him, you'll like Him. He works.

11. God is like Scotch tape. You can't see Him but you know He is there. He is a spirit. We must worship Him for He gives us His love and His power, His mercy, joy, and peace.

The way to receive this message is to be born again. For Jesus said, "I am the way, the truth, and the life. No one comes to the Father but by me." (John 14:6)

Three Men Dying on a Cross

Luke 23:34-43

One died for our sins.

One died for his own sins.

One died forgiven, without sin.

The crowd was railing against Jesus and tormenting Him. He had been beaten and abused tremendously. Yet He prayed to the Father for them and said, "Father, forgive them, for they know not what they do."

The soldiers were unconcerned with His suffering. They parted his garments and cast lots for them.

People stood beholding Him. Some crying, some laughing, some deriding Him saying, "He saved others, let Him save Himself, if He be the Christ, the chosen of God." Soldiers mocked Him, offering Him vinegar to drink.

The repentant thief rebuked his companion and confessed his own sins, declaring Christ to be sinless. He exhibited wonderful faith in Jesus and called Him Lord. He made a model prayer. He received Christ and he immediately got an answer, and was saved right on the cross. Jesus said to him, "Verily I say unto thee, today shalt thou be with me in Paradise." The minute he closed his eye in death, he was in Paradise. To be absent from the body is to be present with the Lord.

He will forgive your sins and save you the minute you repent of your sins and ask Him to come into your heart. You have to believe that He died on the cross for you and believe that He rose again the third day and now is seated at the right hand of the Father.

And He said, "You must be born again to enter into the Kingdom of God." That is a spiritual birth. When you trust Christ to be your Savior and Lord, the Holy spirit comes into you and helps you live for Jesus.

Five Commissions Jesus Gave to His Church

Jesus Christ, the founder and head of the church, made it entirely clear that the principle business of the Church would be preaching the glorious message of the Bible throughout the world. In the four gospels and the Acts appear clear-cut instructions for World Evangelism mandates applicable through the centuries.

1. The Great Commission

And Jesus came and spake unto them, saying, "All power is given unto Me in heaven and in earth. Go ye therefore, and teach all nations, baptizing them in the name of the Father, and of the Son, and of the Holy Ghost: Teaching them to observe all things whatsoever I have commanded you: and, lo, I am with you always, even unto the end of the world. Amen." (Matthew 28:18-20)

From the "Great Commission" we observe that a true church must:

1. Recognize Christ's authority

2. Be a going church, spreading the message of Christ

3. Be involved in worldwide missions to the nations.

4. Win and make disciples.

5. Baptize those who receive Christ.

6. Teach all things Jesus commanded.

7. Be aware of the abiding personal presence of Christ.

These basics have never been aborted. Of course there are constructive social results of Christians being the salt of the earth. The Great Commandment says, "A new commandment I give unto you, That ye love one another; as I have loved you, that ye also love one another. By this shall all men know that ye are my disciples, if ye have love one to another." (John 13:34-35)

It is vital to take a stand for Biblical standards of right and wrong. But these are not our prime goal. Obeying the Great Commission and the Great Commandment go hand in hand.

2. The Go Commission

And he said unto them, Go ye into all the world, and preach the gospel to every creature. (Mark 16:15)

This order is self-explanatory. Nowhere is there a Biblical command to sinners to attend church, although the gospel is hopefully preached there. Believers are individually and collectively to take the responsibility of going with the gospel. Today we need to renew our soul-winning zeal. "He that goeth forth weeping, beareth precious seed, shall doubtless come again, with rejoicing, bringing his sheaves with him." (Psalm 126:6)

3. The Gospel Commission

And said unto them, Thus it is written, and thus it behooved Christ to suffer, and to rise from the dead the third day: And that repentance and remission of sins should be preached in his name among all nations, beginning at Jerusalem. And ye are witnesses of these things. (Luke 24:46-48)

When Paul evangelized the Corinthians, he determined not to know anything among them, save Jesus Christ and Him crucified (1 Corinthians 2:21). Even though Corinth was a cesspool of sin, he knew the only message that could save was the gospel, as he stressed in 1 Corinthians 15:1-4, "Moreover, brethren, I declare unto you the gospel which I preached unto you, which also ye have received, and wherein ye stand; By which also ye are saved, if ye keep in memory what I preached unto you, unless ye have believed in vain. For I delivered unto you first of all that which I also received, how that Christ died for our sins according to the scriptures; And that He was buried, and that He rose again the third day according to the scriptures."

4. The Breathed Commission

Then said Jesus to them again, Peace be unto you: as my Father hath sent me, even so send I you. And when he had said this, He breathed on them, and saith unto them, Receive ye the Holy Ghost. (John 20:21, 22)

Although they were to be anointed with divine power on the day of Pentecost, here they received the indwelling presence of the Holy Ghost or Holy Spirit in fulfillment of our Lord's earlier promise in the Upper Room. Already the unlimited source of power to obey His command, "so send I you," flowed into the beginning, but the filling of the spirit would come later.

5. The Global Commission

But ye shall receive power, after that the Holy Ghost is come upon you. (Acts 1:8a)

He was already in them.

And you shall be witnesses to me both in Jerusalem and all Judea, and in Samaria, and to the utmost parts of the earth. (Acts 1:8b)

These were our Savior's final words before His ascension, articulating the age-long mission of being a witness and spreading His gospel all over the world.

Highway to Heaven, Highway to Holiness

In chapter 32 of Isaiah, he prophesied of the Savior to come, who is the Highway to Heaven, approximately 730 years before Christ was born.

Behold, a king shall reign in righteousness, and princes shall rule in judgment. (Isaiah 32:1)

The highways lie waste, the wayfaring man ceaseth: he hath broken the covenant, he hath despised the cities, he regardeth no man. The earth mourneth and languisheth: Lebanon is ashamed and hewn down: Sharon is like a wilderness; and Bashan and Carmel shake off their fruits. Now will I rise, saith the Lord; now will I be exalted; now will I lift up myself. (Isaiah 33:8-10)

Also,

And an highway shall be there, and a way, and it shall be called The way of holiness; the unclean shall not pass over it; but it shall be for those: the wayfaring men, though fools, shall not err therein. No lion shall be there, nor any ravenous beast shall go up thereon, it shall not be found there; but the redeemed shall walk there: And the ransomed of the Lord shall return, and come to Zion with songs and everlasting joy upon their heads: they shall obtain joy and gladness, and sorrow and sighing shall flee away. (Isaiah 35:8-10)

Isaiah 55 gives an invitation:

1-Ho, every one that thirsteth, come ye to the waters, and he that hath no money; come ye, buy, and eat; yea, come, buy wine and milk without money and without price. ... 3-Incline your ear, and come unto me: hear, and your soul shall live;

and I will make an everlasting covenant with you, even the sure mercies of David. ... 6-Seek ye the Lord while he may be found, call ye upon him while he is near. (Isaiah 55:1,3, 6)

This Highway of Holiness is the Highway that righteous people will take. From the desert of sin's suffering to my Father's House which is the Lord Jesus Christ. Because this is most clearly spelled out in Romans, some call it the Romans Road to Heaven. This Highway is not black topped nor is it concrete, nor is it gold, but it is covered with the blood of the Lord Jesus Christ. For in the 14th chapter of St John, 6th verse, he says, "I am the Way, the Truth, and the Life, no man cometh to the Father but by me." Only those who repent of their sins and ask Jesus to forgive and save them will travel that Highway.

Enter ye in at the strait gate: for wide is the gate, and broad is the way, that leadeth to destruction, and many there be which go in thereat: Because strait is the gate, and narrow is the way, which leadeth unto life, and few there be that find it. ... Not every one that saith unto me, Lord, Lord, shall enter into the kingdom of heaven; but he that doeth the will of my Father which is in heaven. (Matthew 7:13-14, 21)

The Highway to Heaven, or the Romans Road as some call it, begins at Romans 1:16 thru 18. God is the source for the journey to Heaven, power for salvation. We cannot make it on our own, "For all have sinned and come short of the Glory of God." (Romans 3:23) Jesus paid the debt we could not pay. "The wages of sin is death, but the gift of God is enteral life through Jesus Christ our Lord." (Romans 6:23) "That if thou shalt confess with thy mouth the Lord Jesus, and shalt believe in thine heart that God hath raised him from the dead, thou shalt be saved." (Romans 10:9)

The Highway to Heaven won't be found on a map, but a Highway to Heaven does exist. The Romans Road is explained in the book of Romans in the Bible, and it tells how to go to Heaven. The Road begins at:

For I am not ashamed of the gospel of Christ: for it is the power of God unto salvation to every one that believeth. (Romans 1:16)

God is the source of our journey to Heaven. He gives power for salvation to all who believe. We need God's power because we have a problem with sin. "For all have sinned and come short of the glory of God." (Romans 3:23) Sin means missing the mark or missing God's intended destination for us. None of us can reach that destination on his or her own, because everyone is a sinner. When we work, we earn money. Sin earns wages as well: wages of death. Because God loves all sinners, He has provided another route. "For the wages of sin is death, but the gift of God is eternal life through Jesus Christ our Lord." (Romans 6:23)

The Highway to Heaven is found in:

That if thou shalt confess with thy mouth the Lord Jesus, and shalt believe in thine heart that God hath raised him from the dead, thou shalt be saved. (Romans 10:9)

We need to confess our sin and ask God for forgiveness.

To confess Jesus as your Lord involves agreeing with God about your sins and your need for salvation. You must repent of your sin, turning away from the direction in life in which you are going. To believe in thine heart is to place your faith in Jesus, trusting that He died on the cross to pay for your sins. "But God commendeth His love toward us in that while we were yet sinners Christ died for us." (Romans 5:8) If you would like to have salvation in Jesus Christ, sincerely pray a prayer with me:

"Dear God, I confess to you my sin and need for salvation. I turn away from my sins and place my faith in Jesus as my Savior and Lord. Amen."

Then share your faith in Jesus with a Christian friend or pastor. Becoming a Christian is your first step on the lifelong road of spiritual growth and serving God. He desires this for you. Next, follow Christ in Believer's Baptism by immersion and join a local church.

This is the way to my Father's House.

God bless you.

Life and Football

Most everyone likes a good football game, so let's compare our life to one.

You have the ball. Run for the goal line. Your soul is the ball.

First you must decide which team you will play on.

If God's team, you must join first by giving your heart to God by accepting Christ as your personal Savior. By doing this you will be on the winning side.

Paul said in Romans 12 to present your body as a living sacrifice, holy and acceptable to God, which is just a reasonable service.

1. To be on a football team you have to surrender all your time to them.

2. Now you have the ball. Run for the touchdown. Don't look back, you might stumble. You might even fumble the ball. Someone from the other team—Satan's team—may steal the ball.

3. Just as football players must follow the rules, there are rules for staying on God's team and in the game:

    a) Obey the Ten Commandments as best you can.

    b) Clean living, no drinking, no sex outside of marriage, read your Bible and pray, practice your faith.

    c) Go to church. Forsake not the assembling of yourselves together as some do.

4. God is the manager and captain of the team. He is the referee and owner.

5. The Holy Spirit is the coach. He leads and guides and tells you what plays to make to coach you along the way.

6. God is the referee, time keeper, and the score keeper. Don't foul or faint or fall by the wayside. Don't go out of bounds. The way is straight and narrow.

7. You are going against a great power line: Satan and his team. Don't face it alone.

8. Just as football players wear a helmet and shoulder pads, put on the whole armor of God. Pray always that you can stand against Satan and if he takes you down, you don't just lie there. You get up, brush yourself off, and keep going toward the goal line, which is Heaven.

9. Keep going with all your might, for Heaven is the goal and you are saved by the blood of Jesus Christ and by faith. Nothing can separate you from the love of God. We are more than conquerors thru Him who loves us so.

10. So don't fumble the ball, don't faint or fall by the wayside. Keep your eye on the goal. Know the way to victory. Romans 8:31 reminds us that if God is for us, who can be against us?

The Great Homecoming

I was asked to preach at an assisted living home. The lady who asked me told me not to preach on "being born again, as they were all saved." How would she know that? Not everyone who says, "Lord, Lord" will enter into the Kingdom of Heaven. Only those who do the will of the Father.

So I preached on John 14:1-6, "The Great Homecoming". 1 Corinthians 13:12. You have to get ready for the Homecoming by being born again, trusting Christ as your Savior and Lord.

Heaven is home for the saints of God.

1. God the Father is there. He abides there. When we die, the soul goes back to God who gave it. To be absent from the body is to be present with the Lord.

2. Jesus is there, too. He said, "In my Father's house are many mansions: if it were not so, I would have told you. I go to prepare a place for you. And if I go and prepare a place for you, I will come again, and receive you unto myself; that where I am, there ye may be also." (John 14:2-3) "I am the way, the Truth, and the Life." (John 14:6)

3. Heaven is a place where there is no disappointment, no worry, no sickness, no sorrows, no broken hearts, nothing to annoy you, no crying. All will be peace and joy for ever and ever. Not just for a little while and gone, but for eternity.

Also Jesus said, "Let not your hearts be troubled." We are to trust Him in everything, while we are here waiting to go home. He said he will not leave nor forsake us. He would supply our need.

4. Because Heaven is a place of reunion, we'll meet Jesus face to face, and Peter, Paul, the disciples, Abraham, Isaac, Jacob, Moses, etc. All our loved ones who have Christ as Savior, folks we have known. For then we will know as even we are known.

If you are not ready, now is the time. He is the only way possible.

Giving Thanks for God and Country

By G Stanford Pierce, Sr
Clinic Director, Pierce Clinic of Chiropractic

To some, Thanksgiving has become just another holiday; a time of over-eating, napping in front of the TV, maybe some Christmas shopping, catching a matinee movie, or simply a non-event.

But, to most of America, Thanksgiving has been a time of deep reflection on the greatness of our country, the blessing of Liberty, the Freedom to pursue our biggest dreams limited only by our willingness to diligently seek them and gratitude to a Holy God who provides it all.

Historical records reveal that no other nation throughout all the world was ever created with our unique system of laws and inalienable rights for which millions have given their lives to preserve. Time after time Americans have been called upon to stand against tyranny and aggression seeking to destroy our great land and through the Grace of a loving and merciful God, were victorious.

Today, again, our great land is under challenge but this time it is from within. Cherished values of Love, Respect, Honor as well as Faith and Freedom are under assault. Choice is no longer an option but a political mandate. We are being driven to hide God and His Law in church closets and pews while we make federal laws to protect those who choose to be ungodly and unrighteous.

The call once again for America is to stand up for what we know to be right and true and honorable. We must never forget that we are such a blessed people and live in a uniquely blessed nation. The God who guided our forefathers to this great land in 1607 is the same God who poured out His blessing on a faithful nation and propelled her to greatness. Through it all He alone remains unchanged and merits our praise and gratitude for guiding and sustaining us in both times of failure as well as when we rise again unto victory.

This is the real reason we, once again, celebrate Thanksgiving. As you gather with loved ones, family and friends for your traditional food, fun and fellowship, remember to take time to say "Thank you". Thank you to all those who have given so much for your ultimate good and happiness ... and also ... remember to pray for strength to proudly stand for "the Land of the Free and the Home of the Brave, yes, **our** America, "One Nation under God, indivisible with Liberty and Justice for All".

The Seer of Bethlehem

By Stephen V. Shelby

Walking down the street that cool and starry moonlit night
I noticed from the end of town a soft, enchanting light.

Shepherds rushing past me yelled, "Come see, come see the King!"
I pushed and shoved among the crowd and saw a wondrous thing.

The stables standing by the inn were filled with glorious song,
As every rafter, wall, and stall showed forth a heavenly throng.

Wise men, rich arrayed, bowed down with presents they did bring,
And shouts of praise from angels rang, "Hosannah to the King!"

I search the barn both high and low for a mighty, kingly stranger,
But all I saw in the midst of it all was a baby in a manger.

"That's no king," I thought, "It's just a child," when before me all
     things changed.
A hill of death, an angry crowd, the angels no longer sang.

A man before me hung where just before the child was born.
I knew this was the king for now He wore a crown of thorn.

His scepter laid upon his back was a rough and rugged cross.
The blood now flowing from His side showed forth a mighty loss.

I reached to touch the baby's hands and felt the nailprints there,
As angry shouts of, "Crucify Him!" fell upon my ear.

The Mother crying at his feet, where just before she smiled,
The earth was shaking, my heart breaking, for the future of this
     Child.

His best friends would deny Him, a mocking court would try Him,

With hands behind they'd tie Him, and the world would crucify
    Him.

In the raging crowd He looked at Me. I felt so all alone.
The baby smiled, the world grew dark, and the vision then was
    gone.

Within the happy manger scene my legs would stand no more.
I bowed my head, cried tears of anguish, and fell upon the floor.

"Forgive me, Child," "Forgive me, Lord," "Forgive me," I did cry,
For I knew it then, I know it now, it was for me He'd die.

Stumbling out the door I turned for a last look at the Child,
And then I knew my life was changed, He looked at me and smiled.

It's What is Inside that Counts

A pencil maker told the pencil five important lessons before putting it in the box.

1. Everything you do will always leave a mark.

So it is with you and me. Wherever we go or whatever we do, whether the deeds be good or bad.

2. You can always correct the mistakes you make.

We, like the pencil, can remove those mistakes we make. Just turn around and wipe it out and start over. Our eraser is God. If we ask Him, He will forgive our mistake and cast it into the sea of forgiveness, never to be remembered against us anymore. Then we can start over.

3. What is important is what is inside of you.

Without the lead the pencil is empty, no good. And so it is with a person. If you don't have Jesus in your heart, you are dead in trespasses and sin. But if you believe in Jesus Christ and ask Him to forgive you and come into your heart, then you will be able to do the job you were born to do.

4. In life you will undergo painful sharpening, which will only make you better.

Put a knife to the pencil to sharpen it. It takes the two-edged sword of the Bible to sharpen mankind, to perform the job he was made for. It is impossible to please God without faith.

5. To be the best pencil, you must allow yourself to be held and guided by the hand that holds you.

To be a good Christian, you must let God hold you in His hand and let His spirit teach and lead and guide you in all things whatsoever you do if you want to be happy. For you are responsible for you own choices and happiness. It is not up to anyone else to make you happy.

Maybe it will encourage you to know that you are a special person with unique God-given talents and abilities. Only you can fulfill the purpose to which you were born.

Never let yourself get discouraged or think your life is insignificant and cannot be changed.

Remember, like the pencil, that the most important part of who you are is what's inside of you, the Holy Spirit, and let God's hand lead and His Word guide you in what you were born for and what you were created for.

You are special. God created you for His purpose.

Let Him have His way in your life.

You too are one day going to be put in a box. Are you ready to meet God? Think about it. If not, he said, "Today is the day of salvation, now is the appointed time." When the spirit speaks to you saying you are lost, don't say no to him. For God said, My spirit will not always strive with man. Repent of sin, ask Jesus to come into your heart.

How to be 100% Sure You're Going to Heaven

We live in troubled times. This world offers no peace. Money offers no peace. Not even church or family offers true peace. True peace and joy is only found in the Lord Jesus Christ. If you realize something is missing in your life then I ask you to invite the Lord Jesus into your heart. He can give you eternal life. He can give you peace and joy. Jesus loves you enough to give His life for you on the cross. If you ask Him into your life He will come in. If you reject Him, then you have rejected the only hope. The Bible says:

These things have I written unto you that believe on the name of the Son of God; that ye may **know** that ye have eternal life, and that ye may believe on the name of the Son of God. (1 John 5:13)

First acknowledge the consequences of your sin. God tells us what sin does to man's relationship with God.

But your iniquities have separated between you and your God, and your sins have hid his face from you, that he will not hear. (Isaiah 59:2)

Sadly our sins separate us from God in this life, as well as in the afterlife – Hell.

For all have sinned, and come short of the glory of God; (Romans 3:23)

For the wages of sin is death; but the gift of God is eternal life through Jesus Christ our Lord. (Romans 6:23)

Second, acknowledge the sacrifice of Jesus Christ for us. He paid our debt on the cross. God is not willing for anyone to experience eternity without him. Jesus died for us.

The Lord is ... not willing that any should perish, but that all should come to repentance. (2 Peter 3:9)

But God commendeth his love toward us, in that, while we were yet sinners, Christ died for us. (Romans 5:8)

The gift of God is eternal life through Jesus Christ our Lord. (Romans 6:23b)

Third, accept God's gift of eternal life by faith.

For God so loved the world, that he gave his only begotten Son, that whosoever believeth in him should not perish, but have everlasting life. (John 3:16)

We simply need to ask God to save us from our sins. Repent and believe in Christ's sacrifice for us. The Bible says:

That if thou shalt confess with thy mouth the Lord Jesus, and shalt believe in thine heart that God hath raised him from the dead, thou shalt be saved. (Romans 10:9)

Paul said in one of his letters to the churches that we are in the "last days". And if he preached that then, what are we in now?!

We live in turbulent times, but God says, "Come as you are."

If you acknowledge that something is missing in your life, then you should invite Jesus Christ into your life. He can give you peace and joy with eternal life. He loved you so much, He died for you and paid a debt you could not pay. He is the only peace on earth, and peace after death of this body. Heaven could be your home. Choose wisely.

God bless you.

Be Careful

Said to be an ancient Chinese proverb

Be careful of your thoughts ... they become words.

Be careful of your words ... they become actions.

Be careful of your actions ... they become habits.

Be careful of your habits ... they become character.

Be careful of your character ... it becomes your destiny.

Counselling: Communication

Since I am a minister of the gospel, I hope this counselling will help someone to have a better day.

I counsel one this way:

If you want friends, you must be friendly.

Talk to people like you want them to talk to you.

If you speak politely, it is more likely that they will speak politely to you, and they are more likely to listen.

You can catch more flies with honey than you can with vinegar.

Good communication is being able to talk about your feelings and thoughts. It is not always easy to do when one is angry or afraid or nervous.

Communication is a two way street and both people have to work at it.

Spend more time listening than speaking. Most of the time when people have trouble getting their "message" across it is because one or both are not really listening to the other.

"Check out" the other person's frame of mind and surroundings. Is he or she busy or upset or are they free to talk?

Focus on one thing at a time and don't get off track.

Money issues can make it hard to get your real message across. Get your thoughts together before you start an important conversation. Ask yourself what is the main purpose.

Organize your thoughts. Ask yourself what you need to say to this person.

If necessary, write down what you want to say so you don't forget some of the main points to bring up.

Ask yourself if you want to win this discussion or do you want a mutual understanding.

Don't make threats. That may make you feel good to let off steam but even if you don't mean them, they make people afraid of you and could put you in danger. They have a legal right to protect themselves.

Don't call people names, don't curse at them, or talk about them to hurt their feelings.

Don't rehash or drag up the past. New problems will not get solved if you dwell on old ones.

Don't argue about everything the other person says. This makes them angry or feel like you are not listening to them.

Don't plan your response while the other person is still talking. You are not listening if you are planning.

Don't try to read the other person's mind while they are talking. Pay attention to what they are saying instead of trying to figure out what you thought they were saying.

When there is bad communication, it can lead to problems.

Whoever you are having problems with, if you are a Christian go to the Lord together. Pray and ask His counsel. Let Him solve the problem with you. God is your manager.

The Second Touch of Jesus

Read Luke 4:18-19

2 Corinthians 4:3-4

1. The Darkness of the Blind Man

And He cometh to Bethsaida; and they bring a blind man unto him, and besought him to touch him. (Mark 8:22)

2. The Distorting of the Blind Man

And He took the blind man by the hand, and led him out of the town; and when He had spit on his eyes, and put his hands upon him, He asked him if he saw ought. And he looked up, and said, I see men as trees, walking. (Mark 8:23-24)

3. Second Touch of the Blind Man

After that He put His hands again upon his eyes, and made him look up: and he was restored, and saw every man clearly. (Mark 8:25)

4. Second Touch of Disciples

Woe unto them that call evil good, and good evil; that put darkness for light, and light for darkness; that put bitter for sweet, and sweet for bitter! Woe unto them that are wise in their own eyes, and prudent in their own sight! Woe unto them that are mighty to drink wine, and men of strength to mingle strong drink: Which justify the wicked for reward, and take away the righteousness of the righteous from him! (Isaiah 5:20-23)

I believe that there are many Christians today that need the second touch of Jesus, that they might see right from wrong. Because many that claim that they are saved still have the same old habits as before: lying, cursing, stealing, bad temper, selfishness, unkind ways, many others, such as covetousness, greed which is idolatry, vanity which is futile or empty, rebellion, bitterness and resentment, rumbling, complaining, malice, anger, and unforgiveness. As Jesus cleaned out the temple of God, so can He clean out this temple that the Holy Spirit dwells in, if we will ask Him to and submit wholly to Him. He can remove the old habits.

The devil has the spiritual eyes of many blinded, so that things that are sin seem right to them. They need to get the meat of the Gospel, they have been on the milk too long.

5. Declaration of Intention

Maybe some are just hypocrites. Maybe sufficient light was given to believe, but they ask for a sign because they don't want to acknowledge the truth or take responsibility for what they know in their hearts is the truth or right. God help America to get that second touch of Jesus, before it is too late.

An Anchor for the Storms of Life

A big ship can be anchored so it is not carried away in a storm. An anchor is a weight, sometimes hooked iron, that is lowered down in the water by cable or chains to keep a ship from drifting. An anchor is any device that holds something secure, anything giving stability or security. It is something to be relied on, something to have faith in.

Our anchor should be the unchanging Jesus Christ, the Rock of Ages. In this sea of life we are in, the storms will come. Job says, "Man that is born of woman is of few days and full of trouble." (Job 14:1) Whether we have physical, emotional or financial needs, Jesus is peace for every circumstance. Jesus is comfort for every trial, no matter what or when or where. When the storms of life are raging, call on Jesus, with faith, asking Him for help. He would grant it.

He said He would never leave us or forsake us. He will go all the way with us, even to the end of the world. He is security in every storm, aid in every battle, forgiveness for every sin, eventual triumph over every obstacle.

When you have Christ, He will satisfy your deepest longings and bring order, purpose and peace in your life. He will see you through the storm. Nothing else can do that: not money, not a job, and not friends. They tend to forsake you.

What is your anchor?

It should be Jesus. For here is what He did for you.

They took Him before the judge. They beat Him, whipped Him, and mocked Him. They plucked out His beard and spit in His face.

Pilate asked Him many things, but Jesus didn't answer. Pilate's wife told him not to have anything to do with "that just man". The multitude said, "Crucify Him! Crucify Him!" Pilate said he found no fault in Him. But being willing to please the crowd, he had Him scourged and let them crucify Him.

Behold the Lamb. They nailed Him to the Old Rugged Cross, and hammered it down in the hole. They gave Him vinegar to drink and pierced His side. He said, "Father, forgive them, for they know not what they do."

He died. The earth turned dark, the veil was rent from top to bottom.

Joseph got the body down from the cross and wrapped it in clean linen cloth. He laid Him in his own tomb and rolled a stone across the opening. The next day the chief priest and the Pharisees came to Pilate. They said, "While He was alive, He said that in three days He would rise from the dead." So they sealed the tomb and put guards there.

Jesus was dead.

They buried him.

It was a sad time for the disciples and His followers. They had lost their leader, their best friend.

The morning of the first day of the week the ladies were going to anoint Him with sweet spices for embalming

Him for permanent burial. But when they got to the tomb...

He was risen!

He was alive!

The angel said, "He is risen, behold the place where they laid Him. But go tell His disciples and Peter that He goeth into Galilee, and you shall see Him as He said." And they left quickly, with fear and great joy, and ran to bring His disciples word.

Behold the Lamb!

The death, the burial, and the resurrection. The Ascension into Heaven to wait for the returning of His people, to take them forever to be with Him, forever more. Praise the Lord!

The Lamb lives forever more. He is worthy of all praise.

The Eight Paths

I. Paths of Righteousness

He restoreth my soul: he leadeth me in the paths of righteousness for his name's sake. (Psalm 23:3)

II. Straight Paths

All the paths of the Lord are mercy and truth unto such as keep his covenant and his testimonies. (Psalm 25:10)

And make straight paths for your feet, lest that which is lame be turned out of the way; but let it rather be healed. (Hebrews 12:13)

III. Narrow Paths

There are two ways, the straight gate and the wide gate, the way to Heaven and the way to Hell.

Enter ye in at the strait gate: for wide is the gate, and broad is the way, that leadeth to destruction, and many there be which go in thereat: Because strait is the gate, and narrow is the way, which leadeth unto life, and few there be that find it. (Matthew 7:13-14)

IV. Peaceful Paths

Wisdom and understanding is precious.

Her ways are ways of pleasantness, and all her paths are peace. (Proverb 3:17)

V. Paths of the Wicked

The evil way, evil association.

Enter not into the path of the wicked, and go not in the way of evil men. Avoid it, pass not by it, turn from it, and pass away. For they sleep not, except they have done mischief; and their sleep is taken away, unless they cause some to fall. For they eat the bread of wickedness, and drink the wine of violence. (Proverbs 4:14-17)

VI. Shining Paths

But the path of the just is as the shining light, that shineth more and more unto the perfect day. The way of the wicked is as darkness: they know not at what they stumble. (Proverbs 4:18-19)

VII. Plain Paths

Guidance sought.

Teach me thy way, O Lord, and lead me in a plain path, because of mine enemies. (Psalm 27:11)

Teach me to do thy will; for thou art my God: thy spirit is good; lead me into the land of uprightness. (Psalm 143:10)

VIII. Old Paths

God called the Jews to repent.

Thus saith the Lord, Stand ye in the ways, and see, and ask for the old paths, where is the good way, and walk therein, and ye shall find rest for your souls. But they said, We will not walk therein. (Jeremiah 6:16)

Walk in the path of light. Don't stumble.

Follow the Lord in the paths of righteousness to Heaven and life for evermore, as he said in John 14,

or the path and ways of unrighteousness and burn in Hell for ever and ever.

Today is the day of salvation. Get on the right path.

Why Christmas Joy is Short

Christmas joy reminds me of the parable of the sower in Matthew 13. How the joy of celebrating Jesus's birthday doesn't last long: receive the presents, eat dinner, throw out the tree, return to old ways, forget Jesus's birthday.

We should have the Christmas spirit all year long if we've been saved, because the gift that God gave keeps on giving. But with a lot of people, the joy and happiness is just for a while, then it is over.

It's like when the bright lightes are gone and the tree is thrown out, it's like they put Christ out of their homes and lives. Like the emotional hear the word in song, in plays, in preaching, they receive it with joy, but have no roots in themselves. They enjoy it for a while, then the cares of the wolrd come, and weakness of faith, and shallowness of the word in their life. It's all gone. They lose all joy.

The same day went Jesus out of the house, and sat by the sea side. And great multitudes were gathered together unto him, so that he went into a ship, and sat; and the whole multitude stood on the shore. And he spake many things unto them in parables, saying, Behold, a sower went forth to sow; And when he sowed, some seeds fell by the way side, and the fowls came and devoured them up: Some fell upon stony places, where they had not much earth: and forthwith they sprung up, because they had no deepness of earth: And when the sun was up, they were scorched; and because they had no root, they withered away. And some fell among thorns; and the thorns sprung up, and choked them: But other fell into good ground, and brought forth fruit, some an hundredfold, some sixtyfold, some thirtyfold. Who hath ears to hear, let him hear. And the disciples came, and said unto him, Why speakest thou unto them in parables? He answered and said unto them, Because it is given unto you to know the mysteries of the kingdom of heaven, but to them it is not given. For whosoever hath, to him shall be given, and he shall have more abundance: but whosoever hath not, from him shall be taken away even that he hath. Therefore speak I to them in parables: because they seeing see not; and hearing they hear not, neither do they understand. And in them is fulfilled the prophecy of Esaias, which saith, By hearing ye shall hear, and shall not understand; and seeing ye shall see, and shall not perceive: For this people's heart is waxed gross, and their ears are dull of hearing, and their eyes they have closed; lest at any time they should see with their eyes and hear with their ears, and should understand with their heart, and should be converted, and I should heal them. But blessed are your eyes, for they see: and your ears, for they hear. For verily I say unto you, That many prophets and righteous men have desired to see those things which ye see, and have not seen them; and to hear those things which ye hear, and have not heard them. Hear ye therefore the parable of the sower. When any one heareth the word of the kingdom, and understandeth it not, then cometh the wicked one, and catcheth away that which was sown in his heart. This is he which received seed by the way side. But he that received the seed into stony places, the same is he that heareth the word, and anon with joy receiveth it; Yet hath he not root in himself, but dureth for a while: for when tribulation or persecution ariseth because of the word, by and by he is offended. He also that received seed among the thorns is he that heareth the word; and the care of this world, and the deceitfulness of riches, choke the word, and he becometh unfruitful. But he that received seed into the good ground is he that heareth the word, and understandeth it; which also beareth fruit, and bringeth forth, some an hundredfold, some sixty, some thirty. (Matthew 13:1-23)

Man's ignorance, no understanding. Some seeds fell by the wayside, and the fowls devoured them. Through hardness of hearing, careless hearing, and Satan's work, they are unfruitful.

Earthly joy, emotional hearers. Some fell on stony places, where they had not much earth. The message sunk not in, because of no depth, shallow lives, emotional hearers, worldly pleasures. The sun came up and they withered away, instability or unstable, careless hearing.

Some fell among thorns, and the thorns choked them. Things of this life, worldliness, or worldly cares seemed more important, and they produce no fruit in Christ.

Ones who understand and love God's word. Others fell on good ground, they received it spiritually, accepted His word, and brought forth fruit to glorify God. Some 100, 60, some 30 fold. Those who love God and put God first in life. We who do this can have the joy of Christ all year long.

Celebrating Christ's birthday. We seem to cut it short.

2 Corinthians 9:15. God's unspeakable gift. Christmas joy, peace, good will.

James 1:17. Priceless. Everything good and everything perfect comes from God.

Why can't we Christians have the Christmas spirt longer than one day? We are kind of like the Christmas tree, when the bright lights are gone we just throw it away, that's it.

We open our gifts, eat our dinner, maybe say grace first, if somebody thinks of it. Then hurry back to worldly ways. Why not think of Christ awhile?

God's gift is always giving through our whole life and never stops. Look what He is giving us in Heaven.

Nothing in this world compares to what John 14 says:

In my Father's house are many mansions: if it were not so, I would have told you. I go to prepare a place for you. (John 14:2)

Small Demon Inside the Church

Paul saw in a vision a man of Macedonia saying, "Come over into Macedonia and help us."

Immediately they went to Philippi, the chief city of Macedonia. On the Sabbath they went out of the city to a river bank where prayer was to be made. There were Lydia and other women. They worshipped God, and Lydia and her household were saved. They were baptized later. When they went out to pray again there was a girl who had an evil spirit who brought her masters much gain by soothsaying. She followed Paul and Silas saying, "These men are servants of the most high God, which showed us the way of salvation." Paul, being grieved in spirt, said, "In the name of Jesus Christ, come out of her." The same hour he came out. She was no good to her masters anymore. They had Paul and Silas arrested and put in jail. Their feet were put in stocks.

And at midnight Paul and Silas prayed, and sang praises unto God: and the prisoners heard them. (Acts 16:25)

They prayed and sang praises unto God. They had good reason to: Lydia and her household were saved. The young girl with the demon cast out. They were suffering for Christ's sake. They were not angry at the officers or guards.

There was a great earthquake. The foundations of the jail were shaken and immediately doors were opened and bands were loosed. They were singing and praying. I don't know what the song was. It might have been "How Great Thou Art", "Amazing Grace", or "None but Jesus", or whatever. They rang the prayer bells of Heaven.

God showed his great power. Pul stopped the guard from killing himself. It wasn't a jail break; it was God's miraculous deliverance. The prisoners stayed. The keeper asked, "What must I do to be saved?" Paul said, "Believe on the Lord Jesus Christ and thou shall be saved."

God delivered the keeper and his household when they heard the word of God.

Salvation is more than fire insurance! It is life, joy, peace.

Believe on the Lord Jesus Christ and thou shall be saved. Now, today.

Our greatest danger is not the roaring lion or the growling bear outside. We can guard against them. But that small serpent inside slips up on us. Satan's small serpent works on the mind.

Read James 1:26 and 1 Peter 3:10.

It's not the sinner outside the church that splits up the church. It is the little serpents that bite the members inside.

Our homes are destroyed by the same serpents. Our marriages, our lives, all because we don't let God control our entire life.

There is no escape except Jesus Chrrist. He only can stop Satan. Trust Him.

We need to lay aside every weight and the sin which doth so easily beset us, and run with patience the race that is set before us.

Prayer and Faith Will Bring Victory

Therefore I say unto you, What things soever ye desire, when ye pray, believe that ye receive them, and ye shall have them. And when ye stand praying, forgive, if ye have ought against any: that your Father also which is in heaven may forgive you your trespasses. But if ye do not forgive, neither will your Father which is in heaven forgive your trespasses. (Mark 11:24-26)

Faith is honored, and answer, forgiveness, and pardon promised, if you forgive.

And Moses said unto the people, Fear ye not, stand still, and see the salvation of the Lord, which he will shew to you to day: for the Egyptians whom ye have seen to day, ye shall see them again no more for ever. The Lord shall fight for you, and ye shall hold your peace. And the Lord said unto Moses, Wherefore criest thou unto me? speak unto the children of Israel, that they go forward: But lift thou up thy rod, and stretch out thine hand over the sea, and divide it: and the children of Israel shall go on dry ground through the midst of the sea. (Exodus 14:13-16)

The children of Israel feared for life. They cried to God.

First of all, we find 8 steps of faith. 1. Calmness. 2. Quietness. 3. Expectancy. 4. Submission. 5. Prayer. 6. Obedience. 7. Action. And 8. God provides a way.

Prayer is the way to obtain power, spiritual power, from God. Prayer leads to success. If you want to be successful in God's work, you must have faith and stay in the pathway of prayer. If not, you won't have to look far to see why you failed. Prayer brings victory.

Exodus 14:13. Calmness. Fear ye not God's command and God's order. He comforts first, then He removes the cause for fear. God has a "fear not" for all his people, when in trouble, through faith, for he said "I will never leave you nor forsake you."

Quietness. Stand still. When a calm attitude is pursued, the attitude is right for the next rightful step.

Expectancy. See the salvation of the Lord. Faith has a right to expect things from the Lord. Faith will not be disappointed, neither will the Lord disappoint faith. Faith sees the salvation or deliverance of the Lord.

Submission. He – God, not you – will show to you the fourth step to take. Hands off, God will fight for you. Let go and let God handle it all.

Prayer. Moses cried unto the Lord. To be able to pray fervently and effectively requires the soul preparation and a right attitude before God. Prayer digs a well of joy, it brings us nigh to God and brings God nigh to us. There is joy in feeling the closeness of God.

Prayer will open closed doors. Elisha prayed and God shut up the Heavens so that it didn't rain for 3 ½ years. He prayed again and God opened Heaven and it rained abundance of water. Daniel prayed and God shut the lions' mouths that they hurt him not.

Praying is asking God to do that which we are not able to do. He will answer prayers of faith. He can open doors man can't or close doors man can't. Prayer also tenderizes the spirit.

Obedience. God told Moses to tell the children of Israel to go forward. Obedience and faith go hand in hand to get results.

Action. Moses acted on God's command. Action is louder than words. God opened a way where there was no way. God is still in control He rules the wind and the sea. He rules you and me. Our life is in His hands.

Consider Your Ways

It bothers me when I see people shutting God out of their lives, when they are supposed to be Christians. People put pleasure and greed #1 in their lives, after what Christ has done for them. People should read Haggai 1:1-9. They need to ask God to open up the word to them so they can understand. Maybe then they would consider His ways.

The people of that day, Bible times, said they wanted to do God's will. But the time was not right. They had not talked to God about their reasons.

Like people of today, they had become accustomed to only thinking of themselves, so self-centered, they forgot God and what work He wanted them to do.

So when God said, "Consider your ways", He is still telling people of today the same thing, I believe. So think of it. He wanted them to see what was happening to them.

They were struggling under many burdens, but had not stopped to think why they were having so many problems.

God was trying to teach them, but they would not listen. Look at the list of their troubles and see if it rings a bell in your life.

Their crops were small, but they worked hard. They had just enough food, drink, and clothing to survive. They earned money, but it seemed some unexpected expenses always took it away. They could not get ahead. When they brought the paycheck home, it was gone quickly, as if the wind had blown it away.

Do you wonder why they gained so little? They were going about doing their own thing, doing all that hard work for self, for what they needed or wanted. They were doing nothing for God or God's house. So many today are doing the same thing with their lives. They never seem to care, or wonder, or ask God what He wants out of their lives.

God told the people of that day what to do. If they would do it, He would be glorified. He would take care of them and solve their problems. God will do the same today. He is no respecter of persons. I have tried Him, He is the same.

How to Get Saved

If you would like to have Jesus as your Savior, pray this prayer, to Jesus, from your heart, with meaning:

Dear Jesus:

I am a sinner. I ask you to forgive me of my sins and come into my heart.

I believe you are the Son of God.

I believe you can and will save me from a sinners' hell.

I believe you died on the cross for me, arose from the dead after three days, and now you sit at the Father's side as an intercessor for me.

I believe you paid my sin debt, that I could not pay myself.

I want to live the rest of my life for you.

Thank you. In Jesus name I pray, Amen.

I Stake My Claim

By Dwayne Shelby

A wealthy man in the Bible
Had all things that this ole world could give
He didn't have compassion
The kind of love God gives you
When you know Him.
But a beggar on the streets
So hungry his body filled with pain
Had much more wealth in Heaven
On the wings of an Angel made his claim.

I stake my claim in the blood that flows from Calvary
And the promises that God gave to you and me.
No more wandering about
Now I'm sure without a doubt
That on the gold streets of Glory
I'll stake my claim.

For a long time I wandered
Aimlessly without a single trace
That just up ahead of me
I'd soon find that perfect grace-filled place.
It was there God's son was sacrificed
By my sin and he died without blame
So at the foot of Calvary's hill
There I knelt and staked my claim.

You have heard the stories of gold rushes, how they would stake their claims. They would find a few nuggets, and decide where they would take their claim, then go to the place where they had to register, see the man who would put it in writing.

Stake your claim in Jesus and God will write your name in the Book of Life. Then the devil can't take it away. Sealed against the day. You can't be separated from God's love. Then they could go back to their claim and work it, and get more and larger nuggets.

That is the way God does it when we stake our claim in Jesus. The more we work our claim the more God blesses us.

God says, "Try and see if I will open the windows of Heaven and shower out blessings you won't be able to receive."

Jesus Christ was with God the Father before the world was created. He became human and lived among humanity as Jesus of Nazareth. He lived a sinless life. To show us how to live, he died upon a cross to pay for our sins. God raised Him from the dead.

Jesus is the source of eternal life. If you are lost, Jesus wants to be the doorway to new life for you.

Jesus saith unto him, "I am the way, the truth, and the life: no man cometh unto the Father, but by me." (John 14:6)

I stake my claim in the promises of the Lord Jesus Christ. They are as pure gold. Not in Satan's promises for they are as fool's gold, they won't pan out.

What great nuggets we get, blessings from God. Him being our gold mine.

I am come that they might have life, and that they might have it more abundantly. (John 10:10)

After we are saved, faith and works go together. So to get the big nuggets – blessings – we must work our claim. Oh yes, by scratching around the surface you will get some small nuggets, but dig deeper in God's word and work and have greater nuggets.

It seems as there are those in the Church that have not staked their claim in Jesus Christ. Yes, they want the blessings of a Christian, but they have failed to give their body a living sacrifice to the Lord. Yes, they receive some blessings. But he lets it rain on the just and the unjust. But not everyone that says "Lord, Lord" will enter the kingdom of God. It's not his will any should perish, but all would come to repentence.

If ye then be risen with Christ, seek those things which are above, where Christ sitteth on the right hand of God. Set your affection on things above, not on things on the earth. For ye are dead, and your life is hid with Christ in God. When Christ, who is our life, shall appear, then shall ye also appear with him in glory. (Colossians 3:1-4)

But now ye also put off all these; anger, wrath, malice, blasphemy, filthy communication out of your mouth. Lie not one to another, seeing that ye have put off the old man with his deeds; And have put on the new man, which is renewed in knowledge after the image of him that created him: Where there is neither Greek nor Jew, circumcision nor uncircumcision, Barbarian, Scythian, bond nor free: but

Christ is all, and in all. Put on therefore, as the elect of God, holy and beloved, bowels of mercies, kindness, humbleness of mind, meekness, longsuffering; Forbearing one another, and forgiving one another, if any man have a quarrel against any: even as Christ forgave you, so also do ye. And above all these things put on charity, which is the bond of perfectness. And let the peace of God rule in your hearts, to the which also ye are called in one body; and be ye thankful. (Colossians 3:8-15)

Then if you have staked your claim in the blood, do this: Be Heavenly minded.

Some things to put off: Old man.

Some things to put on: New man.

Paul wrote to the Roman Christians:

I beseech you therefore, brethren, by the mercies of God, that ye present your bodies a living sacrifice, holy, acceptable unto God, which is your reasonable service. And be not conformed to this world: but be ye transformed by the renewing of your mind, that ye may prove what is that good, and acceptable, and perfect, will of God. (Romans 12:1-2)

Now is the time. Stake your claim. Today is the day of salvation. Now is the appointed time, when the Holy Spirit speaks to you telling you that you are lost. Be ye also ready, for ye know not the day nor the hour when the Lord will come.

I Stake My Claim In His Blood, How About You?